Then, and Now

Theodore Enslin

THEN, AND NOW

Selected Poems 1943–1993

Edited by Mark Nowak

THE NATIONAL POETRY FOUNDATION

ORONO, MAINE 1999

Copyright © 1958, 1962, 1964, 1966, 1967, 1969, 1970, 1971, 1973, 1974, 1975, 1976, 1980, 1981, 1982, 1985, 1987, 1990, 1991, 1999 by Theodore Enslin.

05 04 03 02 01 00 99   1 2 3 4 5

Published by The National Poetry Foundation, University of Maine, Orono, Maine 04469-5752. Printed by Cushing-Malloy, Inc., Ann Arbor, Michigan 48107.

Distributed by University Press of New England, Hanover and London.

Design consultant: Michael Alpert.

Cover photo by Alison Enslin.

ISBN: 0-943373-53-0 cloth
        0-943373-54-9 paper

The paper used in this publication meets the minimum requirements of the American National Standard for Information Sciences—Permanence of Paper for Printed Library Materials, ansi z39.48-1984.

The publication of this book was made possible in part by a grant from the Stephen and Tabitha King Foundation.

Library of Congress Cataloging-in-Publication Data

Enslin, Theodore.
        Then, and now: selected poems, 1943-1993 / Theodore Enslin; edited
    by Mark Nowak.
            p.   cm.
        Includes bibliographical references and index.
        ISBN 0-943373-53-0. — ISBN 0-943373-54-9 (pbk.)
        I. Nowak, Mark, 1964–   . II. National Poetry Foundation (U.S.)
    III. Title.
    PS3555.N76A   1999
    811' .54—dc21   98-56289

CONTENTS

Then, and Now

from THE WORK PROPOSED

§ ROAD OR RIVER

Wheat, and a river is it?
Wheat,
        A river or a road in
long, numb spirals moving?
By morning, moving gold and
pale star shadows to the sea;
and moving reeds with blackbirds
noon and evening.
                It will move.
Or road will move its pale gold sand—
through fields of coreopsis move its noon.
The night, for river or for road,
will move its silence, and a few
night singers: Crickets, and the wind in wheat.

§ TANSY FOR AUGUST

'Tis not the Object, but the Light
That maketh Hev'n. —Thomas Traherne

And this July—its nakedness burned out—
moves through muffling dust toward August,
down and downward, fire and light obscured
in mist and spent smoke—trails and breathings—
pain and patience in the annealed life
preceding harvest.
                Moves—declares itself
in these attempts: One flower that follows on another—
small this year, and unconvincing.
Withered. Limp. Wrinkled. Corn at midday
offers little. The attempt to sweat
dries salt and stillborn. Brooks run low.

Bogs are, for the moment, dried out, passable and scarred.
Night is their trance—the cicadas
whose patient sound is endless:
Passionate, unsatisfied, and waking.
Trembling, the eyelid closes on a wet, dark, grave;
shuts out the world, retains itself
and dream: The qualities of night.
Night ends—goes up in mist—
leaves at sunrise—lonely and unrested—
solitary on a barren landscape.

The quick star tansy burns itself—sears—pulses
through pace of days set forward through their time—
over the ashes which are fields in drought.
Tansy's bitter buttons hold with heat
their character—the way penultimate for summer—
waking from trance, fever, and July.
Tansy for August. Tansy in the stiff bouquet. Tansy for seed.

§ WITCH HAZEL

This:
That is my straight-flying fury.
And not this:
The dead bone of poetics buried
under sacramental clouds
of sleep or of wine, or too much
awareness of the things that are not there:
Ghosts.

I will make directly through
the woods where the early and late
witch hazel keep blossoms in a long season.
Cut me a switch!
I am not likely to tire on that walk
direct between March and October—
oddly alike and seldom linked—
cut me a switch!

Divined for the water,
the well should be here.
An old cellar hole
dropping away to the infinite
side of the hill and the sunset.
This should be blind water's well.
Switch cut? Very well.

Begin here.
          But straight-flying
is my time of day, and no ruins
but for rocks to build.
Nostalgia is along the way
and very well, but no stopover.

Cut me another switch,
I found that well.
The water is good: Cold
and clear through ten feet
of gravel and sand. It clears
itself.

Cut me a switch to whip old ghosts
through sunsets to the morning.

§ NOTES FOR A COLD BEGINNING

If these snowflakes
   (glad conventions)
mean anything at all,
or those far-fetched geese
   above the cloud
(convened there at matin rites—
   flying south a secondary
consideration having to do with
seasons, as the geese and snowflakes
   do not);
          if, I repeat,

19

these things have any meaning at all,
  and I am here
to record or make what can be
  out of their white and grey
motion: I am alive. It is winter.
And it is a good thing to walk fast
  on a cold day.

§ THE GLASS HARMONICA

It snowed in far country
                north and
beyond the trees.
As I went through the mirror
                my breath froze
clouding it,
        and they saw me no longer
in the villages of spring.
                I walked alone
across level plains,
        and my tracks disappeared
in the snow which went with me.
A wind rose
        playing on harpstrings
and reeds.
        There was nothing there, and my fingers
touched ice.
        A music
                a music
                        an echo of music—
sound not a sound
                in the quiet north country—
the snow.

NEW SHARON'S PROSPECT

A few years after the Pilgrims had founded Plymouth Plantation and the Puritans had settled Boston and Salem, there were a number of books written about this "new" England, usually by men in the employ of English merchants, to attract settlers to a land soon to be exploited. One of the best of these books was William Wood's *New England's Prospect*, a handbook in prose and verse, describing the natural resources, as well as the life to be expected there among the native Indians. Now, three hundred years after, the backwoods sections, particularly those of North New England, have gradually "gone back." In some ways, so have the people who still live there. Seeing it in the hard but close-knit life of one family, I have tried to find out "where they are" in relation to a world that rarely guesses how close to the bone, how careless of what many think "the great concerns" some men still live. In that sense it is a *prospect*.

> Blaze from a pair of trees.
> I see how these are blazing—
> walk that way—
> away—
> and when I've walked away
> from them
> the blaze is there.
> A little fire warms my back,
> stays on this sidehill
> in another's dooryard.

OCTOBER 2. To New Sharon. A family here as biblical as the name of their town. T's father, bent, heavy, but with air of a real patriarch—sire of thirty-two children, living a life we read about, but rarely see. T and I sit in the kitchen with another brother, and The Old Man. The three heads bend at the same angle, impossible for an outsider to duplicate. A common purpose in it—a solidarity there. Archaic it may be, but it is indicative of a life that works—for them. Slow speech, not too much of it, while in the next room the women, mother, daughters, and daughters-in-law sit sewing and chattering.

Heavy,
      slow-muscled,
bent,
he sits near these young men
who swing tough:
An old tree
    with saplings at the foot.

SEPTEMBER 10. Talking with T, my best woodchopper, today. Something almost ferretlike in his look, which is wholly of the woods. He looks down when he talks—a habit with solitary men. His wife comes up with him on good days, and marks the logs for him to cut. Pregnant, she'll be with him until she has to go to have her child. They have two. A third died a year ago of pneumonia—probably in an illheated shack somewhere. Both of them feel this keenly. He says, "It was awful quiet, and I knew it shouldn't be. She was always raisin' hell, you know, kid fashion. And I looked over to her highchair, and she was dead."

THE WIFE

"All loused up"
the world. Yes
all loused up.
   But, would you say so,
seeing her come up over the hill,
eight months pregnant, and heavy,
to bring him a sandwich
                when he had to work so late?

OCTOBER 17. T speaking of his boyhood: "We never had much time for school. The Old Man always had a load of wood to get out, and we had to make up so much time when we went back that we kinda lost courage. One time the truant officer come down to the house, and told the Old Man we'd have to go to school. Dad says, "All right, I'll send 'em, but you might just as well start sendin' down food orders the day I do." He never bothered again.

Sister and I used to cut birch with a bucksaw. We could saw five cords a day, on the yard. Then chainsaws come out, and the Old Man bought one. Bet us a dollar one day he'd beat us with it. I filed that bucksaw blade like a bobcat's teeth, and we went to sawing. We sawed like hell, but we beat the Old Man three to one. Warn't he mad!"

NEW SHARON DOORYARD

If you dig there
scraps of generations
                          broken
will be thrown up.
A hard chance.
                  The dead pine
drops more branches
                        each windy night.

NOVEMBER 3. T's father sits next to the kitchen stove, eyes closed, deceptively drowsy, hat with three toothpicks in the band, pushed back. He rules his clan from here. He raises his right hand: "Madeline, put a stick of wood in that stove." "No wood in the house, Dad, and there's none split." "There's an axe out there. You know what it's for. Josie, feed the horses. The mare'll take four quarts. Hm, can't hear the saw. Stub'll be havin' trouble. I'll see to it. Old Lady, how many wreathes you made?" "Twenty-three." "Make two more, and we'll eat." He gets up, leisurely and assured, and heads for his woodlot.

THE OLD MAN STRIKES FIRE

The eyes washed by sorrow
and the hard life—
by the sun,
or snow in April heats.
Blue in them,
blue north horizon
cold on windy evenings.
His light goes out.
He turns back
to momentary affairs.

OCTOBER 5. The Old Man makes me welcome with a sly peep across his glasses. A prodigal son drives into the dooryard, but dares come no farther. His mother goes out to talk to him, but the Old Man refuses, even though I can tell it's nothing but his fierce pride that keeps him in his chair. He comments, "Well, if he thinks I've changed since he told me I was a damned old thief, I hain't!"

NOVEMBER 17. A crosscurrent of feuds and blood enmity here, but one which no outsider may enter. I would not wisely contradict, or even agree with one who spoke of Old Man T: "He'd get up at two in the mornin' and yard five sticks three miles, if he thought he could steal 'em." T, talking to the Old Man of a comparable exploit, "How come you twitched that wood so far, Dad?" "Well, the horse was standin' there doin' nothin', and the girls didn't have anythin' to do, so I thought they might just as well haul it down."

NOVEMBER 25. The Old Man's House was given him by the town—apparently to keep him at a distance. Even here, such a self-sufficient tribe is considered a danger. Not able to divide their solidarity, the townspeople attempted to isolate it. But the best of the bargain went to the clan. Even in its despairing old age, it is a patriarch's house, with its ancient pegged beams and square rooms—the central entry, low-pitched roof under the dead pine. To the three hickories, and the hopvine that covers one end of the gable—planted undoubtedly by an early settler who loved them—this is a ruler's *homestead*.

> As if it wouldn't stand another winter,
> the hop vine dragging at one side,
> moss an inch thick on the roof,
> sills gone into ground.
>   Outside of the cup.

THE PULL

> Gently, gently,
> all must change
> from what was not
> to this that is/
> is not again.
> Strains as the yoke is drawn—
> one long and level pull.

24

Ah, gently, gently,
whips and curses
break the spell,
and nothing is
as nothing is

DECEMBER 7. T and his father have a deep affection for horses. They aren't always kind or indulgent toward them, but they "look out" for their welfare as they would for one of the family. In summers, they follow the fairs, entering as many of the pulling contests as possible. They do this quite as much to show their pride, as for the "first" or "second money" they usually win. Now the Old Man has a team of chestnuts which he rarely works, but exercises daily. Fair time will come again. T reminiscing: "The Old Man used to drink a lot—home brew we made. Got so he'd have eight quarts a day—two before breakfast, two more at dinner, two for supper, and two after chores. But he was disbarred from the pullin' down to Rome one year. Feller said he was too drunk. He hain't had a drink since. He don't care 'bout us usin' the stuff, but that cured him."

NEW SHARON, NOW

Old bones,
hair combings,
bent matches,
tinfoil,
leavings
all heaped in with ashes.
Kitchen stove crusted
            over.
Have this
            and know:
Untidiness is the essence of despair

THE YOUNGEST

The last of his long line,
she runs slim-legged:
            As a colt.

An old man's child,
but with some of his young fires
breathing.
    She's happy to be alive.
I doubt if she knows this.

 EDE'S BROOK

Seems to have called a halt.
Streaming kettle hole.
The girls with pails
pick their way carefully.
Half the water will be frozen
by the time
they get back to the house.

DECEMBER 12. There is a magnificent well in the New Sharon Dooryard.
Near forty feet deep, the keyed stones hold their position in a perfect circle, as
they have for over a hundred years. A flat slab, at least ten feet across, caps it,
from which the center was cut out round so that a bucket could be lowered.
Admiring it one day, I asked the Old Man about the water. "No good. We lost
two from diphtheria—have to haul water from the brook." Probably genera-
tions of dead cats, or sheer neglect, poisoned it.

THE WELL

To have that water
stoned in by master hands,
the flat top cut for generations
to throw down their buckets,
and still not wholesome,
(mound of horseshit
smoking at one side)
is cursed.
The women walk by,
talking about other things.
Some times they must think about the well,
        festering.

26

DECEMBER 30. T went for a load of hay today—for all of the family horses, but to be stored at The Old Man's under a sagging roof that passes for a haybarn. A cold day, and we were glad enough to get the truck loaded with the coarse, homemade bales. Once arrived at New Sharon, however, the men vanished, and the two youngest girls were left to unload and stack. I could hear a few snickers as the masters rounded the corner of the house—presumably because I chose to stay and help. Probably they look upon me as the Indians did the "squawmen." But it was pleasant to pitch the bales, steady them for Josie, the youngest, who certainly shouldn't be carrying eighty pound loads, laughing at the scratches and sudden skirts of hay and fine snow in the sharp wind. Red, and out of breath, we finished it. Not for nothing all those nostalgic tales of haying. Going in to the fire, I couldn't help feeling that the others, toasting their shins and hands, had missed something.

AFTER THE HAY LOAD

The men left me alone
with the girls
—probably laughing
when I chose to stay with them.
After all, it's woman's work
to pile the bales neatly
in clutter and disorder.
But we stuck at it,
covered with beggar ticks
and straw, from the coarse
fields
        untended.
Laughing a little when a string sagged
enough to collapse a whole bundle,
our faces and hands red
from the cold and the thistles
and
perhaps the close work
                too—
At a steadying chore.

DECEMBER 5. All of T's family will be working in my woods now. Very casually The Old Man asked me if I had much ash to sell. After I'd answered that I did, the talk drifted to other things—a coon hunt, the possibility of more snow. Finally, as he was leaving, The Old Man remarked, "We'll be there in the morning." They will. T went directly home, asking me if I'd come to help him. He wanted to polish the harnesses for his horses. "I'll be working with the Old Man!"

THE CHRISTMAS FERN

A dark morning.
We followed the horses
at a rein's distance
over the new snow
in the twitch trail.
The others were concerned
about the chance of another storm,
but, for the moment,
I was glad that the team
stepped over
a green frond
that had worked free to the winter air.

JANUARY 5. The fear of loneliness, even when we are not physically alone. It is most evident in the women here. They don't have the opportunity to get out—even to the store to talk with neighbors whose "next doors" are often miles away. They pine, these women, turn yellow from loneliness quite as much as from spending the long winters in dark kitchens. They turn "queer" —alcoholic and suicidal—much more easily than their men. I see it, even in the close society that the Old Lady and her daughters have at New Sharon. Perhaps it explains their continuing interest in me—someone "who's been to the outside."

THE OLD LADY WITH HER GIRLS

Sometimes it must be
lonely to the point of a scream
they have in silence—

sitting—talking aimlessly—
sewing—
or just trying to keep warm
by little fires
the men haven't time to tend.

BALDWIN'S MILL

was burned last summer.
The roof had bowed:
slight curve, but unsafe.
Looking at the charred trees there
and the cracked chimney
smothered in snow,
I asked him about it:
"Baldwin come from New Hampshire.
Sawed hard wood there
until it warn't no use."

JANUARY 8. There is an abandoned mill, now a charred millsite, just out-side of the village. Nostalgically, I'm sad to see its swayback "shake" roof gone, after its owner decided that it was no longer safe. (Wasn't it there that I found the little giltframed mirror which I keep in the kitchen?) Asking about it, I had the same answer that I have nearly everywhere here: A case of lost courage. Baldwin, the man who built and ran it seventy-five years ago, "gave up." So much energy, so much *of* men, physical and dream, that lies abandoned in these lean woods. Against that, there must be an integral pitting of forces, sometimes crafty and underhanded, as in the Old Man's tribal strength.

NOVEMBER 22. The Old Man looks out over these hills with the air of a proprietor, and I'm sure he can't think of himself as anywhere else on earth. But the affection he feels for his country is a calculating one, not much given to sentiment, or even curiosity, beyond the living it can afford him. Several times he's asked me the name of Potato Hill, which is my closest neighbor, and when I asked him the name of some of the peaks that one sees spread out to the north of New Sharon Crossroads, he didn't know. Probably he never cut wood there.

When he stands his ground
he's planted,
not without reason.
(Oh
      don't disturb the root.)
But if the breeze touches or stirs him,
he knows it's *here*:
Won't question.
   Won't look up.

NOVEMBER 19. Strange mixture of old New England with contemporary U.S. T lives in a pioneer cabin with his animals around him, but with the latest model chainsaw in his dooryard. He wouldn't start a new job on a Friday, and he hauls his water from the stream. But he can take the engine out of a truck, and replace it as well as any garage mechanic.

A CROSSROADS

He sees strange fortunes in a winter sky
(a dragon's shadow in his stream)
off color by the moon in clouds.
He says, "Blood."
Then looks at the paper,
sees:
     TRACTOR FOR SALE.
chuckles, and fires up,
       "I'll have me that!"

NOVEMBER 1. Shoemakers' children! Often, I go down to T's camp to bucksaw firewood for his wife, while he cuts saleable wood on my east ridge. It seems almost on principle that he never cuts more than a day's supply. Nor is he different in this from most of the woodsmen here.

"All I know"—
It works, in woods he knows as nothing else.
Works on him.
                    He looks up as if to ask a question,
then reaches for his file.
Sure, quick strokes along the sawblade.

THE PEDDLER

"I can tell you, these're good ones—
none of your store boughten apples.
Well yes, a little more'n what they ask.
but look what you're gettin'
I guess prob'ly.

"I heard about that.
                    Say he went off,
left her flat.
No firewood, no nothin'
                    I tell *you*, Mr. Man!"

JANUARY 19. This is still the country of the itinerant peddler—the housewife's friend who will sell her anything: a pair of shoes, a bushel of apples—sometimes at prices below those of the stores, often above the going rate. Sometimes he's a cheat and a quack, but he is trusted and respected. He carries the news, the undercurrent gossip from house to house and that's worth a few extra pennies, even where they're hard to come by. Mary Dalrymple talks about peddling herbs and ferns when she was young, but her old cousin, Johnny Grant, still hawks his wares—even to Mary who's been an adept.

THE EXPEDITION

That day, they were blind to everything
but the distance.
            That made it good.

(When they went for water,
the girls fished out a few cones
from the home brook,
same shape and color as the ones up country.)

NOVEMBER 29. The life is so hard, so impossible at times, that I think these people complicate even the simplest things, fearing that they might be too easy, and so doomed to failure. Old Doris (the Old Lady), several daughters and sons, the Old Man, inevitably, with the small "spotting" axe that he always carries—his sceptre—set out to get pine cones today for their Christmas wreath industry. But not to their woodlot, nor to mine, where plenty of pines grow, but eighty miles to the north, where they filled two small shopping bags.

THE LAST LOAD OUT

We hadn't much time before the mill closed,
and I knew he was afraid of snow.
The leisure in the way he talked,
put knee to log,
            swung it up
into the tier, was without waste.
He didn't say what he was thinking,
but we all knew he was racing
against the wind.
A few snowbirds huddled in the bare elm tree.
He shook his head as he tightened the last chain.

§ PAVANE

for William Carlos Williams

He that asks me what heaven is, meanes not to heare me,
but to silence me. —Sermon XXIII. John Donne

Bending
        over
to look
        at these
dust particles
I think they
                are
held
        by tensions
At first
        I see them
moving
        only as
drops of water
move
        in which
they are
                suspended

My eyes
        clear
to light from above
    then
            to reflection
at the
        bottom
springing
            back
dance—dance beam
the many

dances
the butterfly

large
        as
the palm of my hand

comes under
the edge of the stoop
open
            and black
white edges
                as

an umbrella
someone carried once
for showers

§ SONG IN THE MOOD

Like a flower—like a flower—
or a scream.
                    The door swings shut,
breaks a hand
                like a flower
crushed by a foot.
                    Things become
relevant to all other things—
kinship of being close.
Like a flower—
                    variations
on a better theme.
The snow whitens old ideals
grown dirty
                like a flower.
I want a girl—anyone—
                                sometimes.
Like a flower—like a flower—
mood of a flower.

§

An afternoon
       like this
              too hot to think
I pour water into the stone pitcher
to keep it cool
it helps
     a little
I hear from Bob Kelly
          that
last Sunday
       a pair of handinhand lovers
brought him wild strawberries for breakfast
I look for them here
          in
   two
     (or three)
        days

§

I say there'll be music
        enough
for all of us,
     and poppies
—red-wound poppies bleeding
open cups to receive
thrust after thrust
a violence   disdain at times
tempered
     with what we know
to be there, and
       not enough
to force
   it
can't be put down .

Music and poppies swinging together
you/me.
I wanted to say it one more time.

from THIS DO & THE TALENTS

§ FOR SUSAN, WITH SUNFLOWERS

Although I have never
   seen you
      with flowers / of any kind
I think of you
   and sunflowers
      turning
slowly
   toward the light
      which seems to move
as you do
         kind girl / and fixed
at root
   though moving
      through cold days / and promises
even if they are never kept.
      Our motion / turning
moving
   freely bending
      as this walk / together
moves by light
   the unseen / way.

§ A LITTLE NIGHT MUSIC

Warmth to come home
for a night to

come to
warmth
the hands
come warm to-
gether
touching and healing
joined to
night to come
home to

§ THE BELONGINGS

High,
in your room
I have been sitting quietly
with your things scattered around me:
your love for them is
evident
in their disorder.
That you have used them
displaces dust, and puts them
somehow at my service—
clean, with bright edges,
with loves that are dependent
upon you,
used to your touch
even to your impatient
longing to get rid of them,
all of them, for a moment's breath.
To you they will not seem friendly,
being friends of yours,
and too well known;
but to me they bring a promise
which should be in you—not them—
high, in your room.

I may never
  see your room again,
And this
      is difficult
for me to realize.
I cannot place you elsewhere,
although
    we will meet
in various places
  nervously
acknowledging the fact
    that we know each other.
It would spoil
the things we had together
to remake promises.
  I know that.
You were wiser
        from the start
than I was.
But I make apologies
where I mean none.
We deserve
    more kindness
Than we give ourselves.
To each other
  we were gentle.

TO COME   TO HAVE BECOME

§ TANGERE

And if
    you reach
over

                to touch
whatever it is
you want to touch
if
    ever
          you get to the place
where you think you're
going (headed
in the right direction)
or
    if you
stand right here
reaching over the hip
bone of the little hill
a breeze   slight breeze
being all that you want
to touch really
so long
          as the blaze of in-
tention
          holds up
the fires lit red
                on the smooth wet bark
of pine trees in the afternoon
when the clouds have broken
and the last rays of the sun
are touching
them.

§ THE LABOR

All right
        I'll try
to put down
          a poem
for us.
        You asked me
several times

                    but I
hesitated
            knowing
that it means
                an emptying.
I have ended things
                by writing them
    out.
And we haven't finished
                    (no need
to say
        that I hope we will not.)
What I say
            must be straight
as the line
            between us
has been
            sometimes
the cutting edge
                sharp enough
to wince on
                after the cut
has gone deep
                so
                    hardly noticed
at the moment.
                    You have put
yourself at mercy
                    (mine
will not do)
                the sharing
has been uneven
                    as the times
which
        lopside themselves.
No,
        I cannot be intimate
in speech
            which is for others.

It is not
     the intimate
embarrassment
       of how
you look up
        at the moment
I take you
     but
it is meaningless
       except
in the taking.
        All men
know this
      do violence
remembering.
        All right
it is hard
      when the eyes
look beyond
       without centring
mine
    or yours.
It makes no difference.
          You
spend me
      at times on hurt
decisions
      we will keep them
but not
    as final.
Still, still the marriage bed.
It is not
     consummate
except
     at the moment.
It takes
     doing again.
I say
    doing

and I look
               all
right
             your eyes
are hazel.

§ BALLAD OF THE GOODLY COMPANY: BIRDS

They were singing a grey song
of flat words
               made dull
as the sun between clouds
                              wading
down the afternoon
                        now
this morning   the rain
                           makes
such a racket between
                         the eaves
and discarded metal
                        in the dooryard
I can't tell what song
                          from
the color of the day
                         I would say
some shadings
                  up
from green.

§ 3/25/65

not peace
and there is
            a deep estrangement
between their lives
                     and how I live but

42

the hollows of my eyes
                    are deep
they may not hold
                    the usual sorrows
or a casual reference
                    to death,
but something hides there
                    which is
uncomfortable and
                    not peace

§ MUSETTE

Do not be sad, my girl,
that so much snow has fallen.
Around us and beyond,
                    it touches
briefly
         on the bitter scars
that summer left;
                    lies in the angle
of the wall
         where we left tansy
for our coming year.
                    Another wind,
another cloud
         come fresh across our lips and
we will taste the root of love
itself
         when there is sun again.

§

the wrinkled cheeks
of the apples
of the countrywoman
gathering them
frozen

§ SPRING NIGHT, VERMONT OLD STYLE

So that
    the door   almost a gate
swings shut
    the gable end
a second storey entrance
        possibly
for apples or onions
       it creaks a bit
stiffly adding
    sound
barring and subtracting
the late moon
    setting
behind the ragged hill.

§

al ign ment
order
remade
    these
disparate
    things
light
    five candles
one swift curl

                    incense
        smoke
                    destroys
                                serious
            intent

§ SONG OF THE JAIL'S REJECT (*his voice*)

Do not
        (*As you walk into the room,*
the room changes.)
                    pity or humor me
with kindness.
                    (*The room spins.*
Around me are no fixed things.)
                            I accept
your warmth, but not as you give it.
                                (*I see*
you come up to me, singing.
                        What do you see?)
It is not brave to say of suffering,
that what is noble suffers long.
                        (*Be careful,*
there is heat that threatens to destroy us,
        as my lip to yours
                    touches and retreats.)
A long time
        being.
It is only the beginning.
                    There. You may claim my hands.
(*The room is clear once more, set in its own order.*)
Take both of them—my hands are useless to me—
inept,
        which you think are my tools.
You have only the outside of a private ritual.
(*The room is yours, and I am part of it,*
happy, for the moment to be among your things.)

45

By not doing

        you could take and cause darkness.

(It is closer now than bearable, and yet I seek you out.
A man's seeking

        is its own fulfillment.)

It is unlikely.

        I stand wholly free of you.

                (My love.

It's a poor thing, but all I find to give.)

I am touched in madness.

           (fades—

You will leave the room again.
It is too much to keep for long.
It fades.)

        My silence.

§ HOT ROD

Among the tall yellow flowers
(ten petalled helianthus)
he works over the rusted body,
greased rods of a cut down truck—
something he made for himself.
He grins,

        wipes his hands
across filthy dungarees,
walks back through the flowers
without noticing

            them.

§ OF POEM

That others have written their poems
this year

        that a sense of poem
runs through river beds drying

in late dry season
                    that I might
come to the wound of love
                        write my poem
is possible as spent shot
pattern of shot
               the deer's wound
leaking bright blood
                      rich into brown leaves
or later against snow   its smooth cheek
A bright blood rising   there   in the moon's shadow
flush
            and the eyes looking out
from acute danger
                    mine as the eyes of stalked prey
flushed.
            As the poem is startled from sobbing
the throat held tight in its first desire to speak
remains still   .
              It is the poem of silence
which breaks it.

                The poem is written on slag
on the side of the tree facing sleet wind
crusted and scaled
              broken into eventually
shattered but holding for thaw its lament
only
       as wind is the speaking
lament in the scrape of the branches
frozen
     dry.
          And the poem
is written on ground   or on worm casts
the breaking of seed   the broken hull of a waiting .
Men wait and regret   and can't know that they wait
                  for the poem
are confused for their want of it
waiting with chins pressed
against knees

cane for support
the dry weight   .
Poem comes through   they complain of the dust.
Poem is written on water   without it.

The poem
needs not be written
it is/
/is not
as the turn of a head speaks its love and is known.
Cannot lie.
It is poem that has written on entrails of fish
a warm breath.
It is poem as welcome
as going.
We have written   but only as poem bids write
to where standing
we are   .

§

If I have loved her well and strong,
god knows, I have not loved
her well enough for whom she is.
No matter how I turn to her
the sense that I should give her more.
The love I gave
is but the token part
of what I feel.
That she deserves me more,
That I must give it
as she is.
Her presence—
that I know she is
makes me more able.
Still,
I feel at loss.

I

It is this place
that you look for,
and you find it:
well-watered by
a brook called stream—
almost, but not quite,
a river.
              The stream, then,
is the pulse of the
town-
          ship,
including the village,
and certain outlying
districts—
              most of them
abandoned
              except
for vicarious life
in the easier months.
The stream begins
above the town
              lines
in a number of bog ponds,
carries down and out of it
a sediment
              almost unseen
until the dam
              at the mill
fouls it and
              traps it,
and then releases its sludge
to another town
and a river.
It is the back
bone
of the place

now,
        though it
is no longer
            important
in the sense that it once was.

        11

There is the village
                proper,
and a few fanning roads
which soon die
in the leaves—
            overgrown
as the fields
        of the old men
who left themselves there—
sweat dried on the rocks that
still might lick salt,
if you knew how to find it.
Following the stream of water,
a stream of houses,
            decaying
in most cases—
            the barns
fallen in,
        and the chimneys
crooked
        and faulty.
The men who live here
take to the woods
            early,
or disappear.
            They are
crabbed in their survival,
gnarl early,
        carry
themselves to their graves
in poverty
        and harshness.

III

Above the town
lie its mountains—
ravaged by over-
cutting:
          dark growth,
and hard wood,
But the mountains are open
in their sleep and
                    aloofness.
They heal better
          than men.
They contain bits
          of the life
that sticks to them—
                    wild—
and the tame remnants—
cellar holes,
          walls,
an axe-head
          or two,
wagon-tires,
          where deer
and other free lives
                    nose through them
for berries.

IV

But the life of the men
casts a shadow
          even
across the sun—
there is something
                    that bitters
even the best days.
                    It will not
rub out.

When you first come here
you will not notice it,
then time
            drives it
home
            like a nail
into bone.
There is sadness,
and desperate
                  hatred.
In the close-in
                  of winter
it becomes
                  unbearable.
The wind is a scream—
a pain
            that bears gossip—
that act
            of those men
who have nothing to do
except curse that same nothing.
It will pass.
                  There is brightness,
But the ache of the land
comes up
            time
and time again.
You have found
                  the town
that ends the road,
but it finds you
                  as surely.
In your love
            of it,
you come close to its horror,
and cling there.
It will murder you
in the end.

This comes back to me:
A chance word from a letter,
later put down by me
as something not quite genuine:
that
      'you don't divide life—
not wisely.'
          Now, in this kitchen,
sitting with this woman,
reading the book of poems which
                    a friend sent me,
(with that quotation)
          I look up
and smile at her, my friend,
know, that as this room holds many things
and love itself,
I spoke the truth.

§

A direction.
      I turn to it
wondering if it is exact.
I know
      each time the light breath
of the wind
      stirs
against my cheek—
          first
one side
      then the other
as if fingers
      stayed there
briefly

§ TO BE AS THEY ARE:
A DANCE
REPOSE IN ERUPTION

for Robert Kelly and Stan Brakhage

the room
            lights up
the carpet.
                  We can bear to wait
but not that long.
                        It is time at fault,
our sense of it the root.
Thank god for peace,
                        and now,
and
      at the hour of our death.
The sense of it.

§ TO COME   TO HAVE BECOME

To say the least is
                  perhaps
to say everything—
                        the slight gesture or
inflection—
                  voice that rises/
/falls.
            The pause between each breath—
one   which passes
                        each to each,
an instance of our lives.
                        The least
becomes our life and
                  much more.

What falls/
                fails
is never certain
wavers
            I
see
    darkness
in it
        crumpled
pinched
            impression
as my breath takes it
stiffening
            the nose hairs
a shrub of ice
                beginning to form.
It may not fail
                I can tell
only by an occasional
slap in the face
                wind
but no stinging
                too soft.
Well,
        I have been walking
and my eyes are unaccustomed
to darkness
            particularly
this which is not half light
                        but
incomplete.
            I resist it
all change becomes an outrage
to know it
            I go out of it
switch on the light
                in here

see what happened
                    by my sleeve
before brushing it off.

                    §

It may please you to know that
I have been looking through things
which in some ways have touched us.
The air of detachment is missing
with which we came to them, and
perspective lends dimensions
uncomfortable at times, but there is more
to them than simple remembrance—
trophies or souvenirs.
                    They are
a part—
          the weave constructed
below the outside   unseen but present
as we were present blood to blood—
sharing the same drawn breath.

                    §

          Feather for feather—
only
          all I had
was a dry leaf
from a tree by the Art Museum
in Portland,
          and it was
too old and dry to be handled,
so there are feathers and leaves
both here
          and not here.
It is a sad world.

I've heard this,
but think only the men are sad
who live in a world
where
        feathers
leaves
        all light things
whirl up
        and are caught
in the face of the sun.

§ APPLE TREE STUDY

So bright—
there is fever in it.
Then the weight of color
turns to light,
            rises
in waves of incense
falls
        away.
And one sharp wind
climbs through
                and over
shatters
        in
one
        sweet
    storm

§ THE WORDS—THE MUSIC

Looking again
at your poems
—all of them—
that lie in the folder

of your work,
                    I feel
a great clean breeze
that sweeps there—
                              through
to me—
              laying me open
to the stars,
                and silence
which becomes our presence
in it.
              It will make no difference
if men pass by them
              and do not see
the things
              made evident,
nor if the strength behind your words
flows
          like a mountain stream
unharnessed.
                    These words of yours
are present,
                and the world behind them waits.
One day a song
                    will come
from them—
                a hand
that touches gently.
In these two things
the time
          will turn
to better time,
and live
          for those who hear
and know these words.
                          They will
not be chained to books,
or casual acceptance,
but come,
              as they

are coming now:
                    Running
and leaping,
                    slow walk
and high flight.
                    They will hold
their ripeness,
                    surely,
as their love—
                    my love.

                    §

so that
            if I wanted
to
      I could go to
the window
                    and look out
where you have been
                              see
you there
                    why is it?
we are sitting quietly enough
with books
                    two cups of tea
nearly finished
                    (if you like
i'll heat more water)   .

                    § P. S.

Let's wait for night—
the day has been a lonely one.
Letters I didn't send lie on the table,
waiting.

I hoped you'd come here, but you didn't.
I couldn't see the hills clearly,
looking at other things,
trying to fill time writing these letters.
(Soon I'll take them down and mail them.
They'll go out tonight.)
Then I'll close the door and wait for you
in large, dark shadows.

§ VIOLETS—RAILROAD CUT

Although I am tempted,
I will not pick these
                    —blue—
The color
            (or is it the flower?)
turns a sadness
                in you.
After the rains that
                    beat them
but
    brought them out,
they are in this place,
and I will tell you about it:
Under a raw bank
on the line
            you will find
a skyful
            in a ditch.
If you want them,
                    I will go back
there.

§ SONG

To go alone
   into that wood
chance reading
   fire in stones
the mist that drops
   along the ground
to go there
   openly
not lose the way
   talking to bird
or branch
   red-budded
alone to hear it
   silence
as the measure
   walk to love
where two alone
   are not
that too

§

'Between',
      you say it
as if it meant
      one thing
which holds some others
together:
    that
which is between us.
But it does not come exact.
Between
     implies
the bad-luck tree
        di-
viding lovers,

                              or the wedge
              between forced grains of wood—
              a mountain in the foreground
              losing valleys
                              whose still air
              lies in frost
                              far to the north
              from where we see.

                              §

              Not that
                              the reprieve in itself
              is important.
                              True,
              it takes away pain,
                              brings sun
              light
                      clear to us—
              but that the force which binds us
              works no ill
                              that love brings
              peace
                      to us
                              that we are granted
              whom we are.

§ THE NIGHT WITH FIGURES

              I see you moving.
                              My eyes
              are closed.
                              At least they close
              on you
                      and fix you
              in this room.

What is it you are saying?
I hear through color
textures of the words you use.

That things grow from us which were once between.
That this breath hesitates.   We draw it from the
                         winter silence.
That these echoes are your footsteps, echoes
                    which merge with mine.
That these things struggle for the light, like
                    blind trees in blind sunlight.

It is enough for the present.

These things are.

I see you moving
                    my pulse
has caught the sense of movement.
The stir of you in sleep
has said it.
          Not a word
escapes you.
               Not one word
goes past me.
               Yet I hear you—
hear you out
               in long slow lines.

1961–1966

from THE DIABELLI VARIATIONS
& OTHER POEMS

§ THE LOG OF THE DIVIDED WILDERNESS

In the dark mind, secret came by wind
roiling hot over the far deserts to the wall—
the slow speed and the whisper-silence,
the rock falling into the deep well—
widening, tremble, and quiet.
Wisdom? Perhaps. Space. Breadth between suns,
stars and madness.
                    Unknown lit
shadows moving in light across the black sides
of moons—spun into orbits not their own.
The wind will not return to the hot deserts.

As

in the autumn, after the others had come in,
one cow calved, and licked her wet charge
into life.
                    It stood unsteadily and trembled
to hear the first whirl of falling leaves.
Snow was early that year, and the young calf
dozed in the warm steam shrouding his safety.

And

there were men walking, the flow of them
beetling, wedging the distances.
(Some called it marching, but men walk,
spurring themselves
                    by wind.)
The land is scarred from their walking.
A stir of old leaves covers the split rocks—
The deep channels of walking—and the sand
stains certain tides with blood.

Then

       the women quarreled. The river fled their shadows—
       kept them—.
                  All that day there was talk
       echoed, washed out. Lost.

Now

       let us speak with some sort of wisdom
       of the church—in going—the movement of wind,
       and the relentless companies of visitors (never those
          who stay).
       The idea rubs off, and the hush is so much dry corn
       rattling in the winter's sleet.
                       There seems
       to be no renewal. But to move on—
       an awareness. Heat and sweat. An old shirt
       hung over the fire to dry—
                   (the passion, slack
       in its limp fold)
                its rightness.
       It cannot die out of what it had.
                       So, roasting a chicken
                       for supper.

Later

       the man (myself) sat thinking the dust was laid,
       only by hurricane was drought ended
       and that the elders had said nothing about that and
       the first ripe elderberry (raw) was a good dessert
       to breakfast

But

       now what is it happens?
       A man follows fashion—he
       chokes his throat or leaves it free, not
       because he cares what it is himself;
       People talk.
                  A man can write so;
       GOD DAMN THEM! Let talk go.
       I have dropped ballast, deck load,
       centerboard before now. And travelling,

I still go.
The journey goes on
(wheeling around.) A wind off shore.
Count flashes.

Next

I will bind your eyes.
(Silk. And silk is cast off—
ha! Samarkand! Show me down to hell;
bring me back, but it will
not be two dead maple leaves that fell
in August. Or children walking in dusk
to water—wading—cranes in silence, and the rings of
charmed breathlessness—burnished heads against
the sunlight fading—the slow speech and laughter.
Then do! Bind up our eyes in silk.

As

I was thinking:
(thought being as I plucked corn)
it took the blackbird so to maim
and gouge.
No seed too good for him.
It was shrill in all his character
its hinge and filed-on iron.
Less corn, more blackbirds in a field.

At noon

a piece of daylight fell on water.
(No one heard it.)
Its shaft struck deep where fish
swept oiled and smooth
through silver—darkness and the cold
of ageless character.
But it was daylight falling there
that bent one slender ribbon reed.

The Night

Night brushing at the face of things,
but night wrapped up in fog,
wadded in it, a darkness tempered by the sea—

a grey ghost thin, with blood
dilute and pink—the nerve exposed
and pounding. Visible to us.
Dreading it, we watched. Such anguish
as those gods must know!
                              Only the scale
of silence here: The drip from trees.

To

where the sky swings inward
cold, and over mountains, came the herders
driving antlered forests from the north.
And someone asked an old man
rimed with winter how he fared.
"Well enough."
                    "How many reindeer in your herd?"
"Count them!"

Children

there are fairy tales from the wind tonight.
(Do you know "The Skittering Oak," "The
Bashful Elm," and "The Shy Stars"
or "The Raging Forest with Black Teeth"?)
Or sanctioning what for immediate concern, what do
     you know?
What can you tell us at the campfire? (or none for fear?)
Not to brush our teeth, I trust.
Manners? Good, good God we have none!
Let us rise. Let us sing. Make a joyful noise.
"Tumult" is a good unbeaten word for it.
Tell us how a golden prince found a golden princess
in a diamond palace where some spread emeralds
under alabaster windows, charmed by snakes,
and we were able to breathe pure air,
and live.

Once

I found a black feather
after I had seen the crow flash down,
as if in water, to rend some carrion heart
deserted by the proud first

67

who stalked.
                    A way of getting on;
but the yell of jackals is in the poisoned air:
Carious, green, metallic.

Freed Slave
          and feral as a beast, he ranged in moonlight,
          hungering and quick as thievery;
          the circle-flying arms played quickly
          at his purpose.
                    Before the
          sun struck earth full-force,

          or bladed to the hilt the sea, the man
          had vanished, leaving raped lands behind him.

Samson,
          the slayer of wild beasts, and of men,
          is dead.

Isaiah,
          the prince of the prophets,
          is dead.
                    But the man is not yet
          dead, who spurns the catalogs of greatness,
          which sound only as the bone singing in dry
          winds where dust blows out the fertility
          of misused fields, and mourns by the sharp-spined
               windrows
          against lee shores.

Falling
          Stella Maris. What star was that?
          One hissing in the sea as quenched as coal.
          (Ashes and embers turn up daily at low tide;
          the water limned.)
          No pharos for the sailors: Winds and prayers.
          There is rigging set for storms—no peep beyond the
               clouds.

Here are

       the graveyards counted as the stones.
       Listen! There are sea-ghosts walking,
       and outside, drowned men stride through
       clear water—tides are waist-deep to them—
       cold matches cold. Blue open eyes
       stare fixed at round horizons. Lank as brown kelp
       their wet hair streams; lashed to the wind
       as living are to masts, they howl lost voices
       and go on journies shipped
       with stars, cold fogs, and snows.
       The voices are of mews and petrels, and the lost.

In wisdom

       was the sure, divided heart,
       it was an army, but it was a man.
       It was the dark of winter muffled.
       It was glory. Or defeated as the spent storm,
       ragged as the moon-struck sea,
       (or held in fief). It was the will against,
       and the assent, the hammer beaten
       as it swung, no pendulum in time
       waves in the desert waters,
       secret and released.

At harvest

       witch hazel, and those late-mingled branches
       years, and a year caught so—
       oh, skeins of hair, straw spun to gold,
       the barns burst open—straw and apples—
       midnights lost on sightless roads;
       and water, oceans by convection, washing down
          men's sleep.

In rains,

       these are nails of silver which
       peg our death,
       rise brooding, on the backs
       of fields. Our naked flesh
       to nerve and chipped
       agonizing bone:

Leave silver-studded heads
for all to see,
whenever sun turns light again.

Concluding,
      it was dark, and all the rivers of the world
      gleamed black, parting the desert lips as inch worms
      glorying at sun on grass. So lengthened and was still,
      the wind caught wisdom-wise
      and secret as the place of a beginning.
      Soldiers, battles, women quarreling,
      dead and departed, a very world of stillness.
      Only the sea ran red its memory down kelp
      and over sand.
                Tides are not limbo,
and only one man at beginning was a drowned man
lost at sea.

from AGREEMENT, AND BACK

§ THE FOUR TEMPERAMENTS

I

SANGUINE

Reasoning this way:
              although there are few
reasons to believe it—
              there *is* hope.
The things which are usually one way,

can as well be
          another—
as if one took
          something from one pocket,
put it in another,   and

said nothing about it.

Briefly,
       failure is no reason
to believe in failure,
                or that the rule
applies.
        It takes a longer vision—
a breath drawn

without hesitation.

Sometimes it is good to stand at a distance—

the distance reveals something
                  if it is only
more distance.
          But the reason is not

in form of propositions,
              it must open
from a spontaneous feeling

—combustion—
           no—a bit strong.
Looking through these windows

at that street
          the doctor's word is
one
      to remember:

"While there's life
            there *is*
      hope."

If I require little,
                it may be
my strength:
                To sit as rocks do.
The snow and the rain may fall

over and around me.
                        If frost splits my shell,
why,
        that's all right, too.
I am not disturbed.
                    It puzzles me
to see the will that man has.

He rakes his leaves today.
                            Burns them.
(I enjoy the smell of burning.)

He'll have to do it again tomorrow—

so—
I am not worried at the leaves here.

It pleases me to think over
the possibilities of what I *might* do,
                                and then
do none of them.
                I know what they say.
I'm lazy.
        So what?
A hundred years from now
                        we'll all be
at peace.
            My ease will be more extreme than now.
But no more so than theirs.
                            A levelling.

I wish all things were level.

                    I mistrust mountains.

There are things I dislike,

                but none
is worth an argument.

I do take pride in this:

                I am a good neighbor.

III

CHOLERIC

The *way* of looking!

A man had better not cross me.

Flat on the face of a shovel

              and
just as hard.

           I might not take offense
but there is the old rattler's motto:

"Don't tread on me."

The right way to live—
and all this laziness:

The world is vibrant—

take what you can

             and crack it
with the hardest jaws.

Muscles are for use.

I knew that one night—

               in a rage
pushing the car into the road

out of a snowdrift
          that needed
two men with spades.
(A deflection from where the rage was felt.)

Always the feeling of youth—

that so much energy must
                    reach out and
touch someone
               before my head splits
open
        like so much straight-grained wood.
How many times I have asked

and been denied

more force where it is needed now.

Now!
            as if there were any other time.
Never—
          and completion of never.
Watch out for me.

I don't give up easily.

IV

MELANCHOLIC

If there were someone to talk to—

for a moment—
                one breath—
but no—it all ends here

in my throat,
            my teeth
biting back the salt and blood.

74

Contained:
        I have become worthless,
thrown out—
              garbage in an untended alley.
To sleep.
       The nights are hardest—
but days—
          for sleeping as well.
If I had the courage—

but death is not courage.

It ends again—

this time on a scream.

It lies in the crippling

of inactivity—

what reaches me

as an unreached conclusion.

It has ended,

and it never began.

Sweat that comes out yellow bile

to soak tainted
into already drenched sheets.

I should make that call.
                  Speak to my friend,
who will say,
        "yes, yes.
that is how it is.
           I know.
I have been there."

Finally,
"But I can't help you

anymore than you can help me."

And it all ends again.

If there were someone to talk to—

from **THE POEMS**

THE FIRE POEM

I

Note that the fire
    consumes not itself,
but what is cast there:
                Into it.
    or
Note: That the fire
              consumes
only what is brought to it.
            Note
from Eckhart, who had watched fires,
warmed body and spirit there
—spiritu in corpore—
             who had seen
clearly that the natural life
            relates
to the divine
        or given
    through
not always a correlation.
It is dangerous to assume
          the ecology

of these things.
                              But it is the time of fire
and its sometime fuel.

                    2

            That at night
            the fire
                    sinks
                            down
            is rescued
                    only
            by the morning log
            in nick of time
                            to
            renew itself
                    go out
            through radiance
            the high intention
            glowing/
                    /in fruition.

                    3

            At Twelfth Night's burning
            of the greens
                        there is
            more than cleanliness:
                        To destroy
            more than the ritual implies—
            some old urge
                        ancestry
            to show the face of one man
            to another
                        in the darkness.
            That fire purifies
                        is no mistake:
            fructifies
            nor that it claims the sun

light
    in a little place—
this hard-cored-coal.

4

But to break loose again—
the finger length
       flame
following
      underground
the source of roots—
suddenly
     whirls up
catches in the high trees
a crown fire
      rising
with the wind.

5

or one
small
votive
light

6

Whatever gives
     gives back.
It is not the lesson of the fire
more than what the fire heard.
It would be this
     at a season
—narrowing it to self—
       when I might sit
before it with my love,
and we should know

by how the light
　　　　　struck
from our eyes
　　　　　—the glow of skin—
these dim reflections
　　　　　　from which
we joined ourselves
　　　　　and held our own.

7

The fire consumes—
but not itself.

§ THE POEM OF NO SHADOW

1

Shouldered this pack—
wanigan—
　　　　　supplies
for three days walking,
and I walked it
straight.
　　　　　The center had been reached
by the turn of the day.
The slow seed of the rain
continued.

2

At that time I rose
light
from the soles of my feet,
dressed
　　　　　(or did I lie down
full-dressed? knowing

79

that I would rise
so?)
But rising
                somehow
out of the knowledge
that preparation had been sleep.
that I had lain there
irresponsible
to assume this later form
in rising,
                I went out
and took full air—
the morning's light ahead of me—
and darkness catching at my heels.

3

I took these things with me,
which rubbed out smooth
by travel,
and the lumps of darkness vanished
where I cast no shadow in the light.
I wondered:
                What has changed me?

4

I began—
but I found there
no beginning,
                nor as an end
a period—
                finality
was no part of it.
The human condition formed
in clusters—
                grew upon the vine
as grapes,
and at any point

                                    picked up
it involved the rest of it—
totality
               which was more
and less than
        total.

                        5

To speak of reflections
is not to speak of this journey.
There was nothing
but the direct falling
(and rising)
                        heat.
No shade.
It was the sun
and the focus of the sun's heat
which assailed me.

                        6

Things being what they are—
it equals
what we are.
The appearance
and the skin
speak directly
of the center of things.

                        7

The wanigan:
In which I carried
all that was mine,
made my essential
purpose.

It was an end in itself,
an end in view
as
the only end.

8

I impinge upon this rock.
I do not shelter there—
the spring opens
from the earth,
but it is the earth.
I have entered the water,
and I become it.
The water becomes myself.

from THE COUNTRY OF OUR CONSCIOUSNESS

§ CANSO

*—It is said that cannibals dislike
the taste of flesh tainted with tobacco smoke.*

1. Now I guess
   I'll fill things up.
   The water thawed
   at ground level.
   The use of water
   various—
   its goings in
   its comings out
   to cloaca maxima
   and clears
   in ten feet of
   gravel
   or

sand
straight run.

2. But mirrors
    make doors
    one hinged
    on the next one.
    Entrances
    are difficult
    exits
    impossible.
    I am writing
    a poem to hold things
    that are separate
    usually
    the poem
    in front of the mirror
    a basket
    of tight-woven wood
    and
            its reflection.

3. The boy leading a goat
    up the road
    in the middle of winter
    gives an impression
    of other places—
    weathers
    not so sharply made.
    He walks quickly
    while the goat
    splays her feet
    turns eyes
    like candied raisins
    first one side
    then the other
    looking
            looking
    vacantly.

4. It may start
    in the agony
    of an unlucky
    number
    such as
    13
    but if it con-
    tinues long enough
    14 follows
    which is
    twice 7
    the perfect
    and indivisible
    number
    of the ancients
    can be carried
    to 49
    equals:
    7 x 7.

5. No, and I didn't
    want to write it
    the way it came out
    it was in
    words which were
    symbols
    sometimes elegant
    images
    often gilt-edged.
    How to say it
    or write it
    the gentle pressure
    love
    presuming itself
    to be insistent?
    How I look across
    how my love
    looks back.

6. It's a hard morning
   in which
   to do anything at all
   about nothing
   at all.
   I've tried
   long enough
   with a will
   which is detached
   as if my eye
   were in several places.
   Several minds
   or several strengths
   have been here
   perhaps to weaken
   the attempt.
   Let not your left
   know what your right hand
   is doing.

7. And if the flower
   flowers
   let it by all means
   in itself
   flower.
   It is so
   near the spring
        that frozen wood
   springs apart
   its frozen buds
   at one look
   from the sun
   scarcely a nod.
   You know
   Where I am tending
   what it was I
   started to say
   which cannot finish
   the poem

                    in its
        deed
             does not.

§ LISTENING TO MOZART

                    I

        ALLEGRO ASSAI

I have often thought of this music
in certain ways:
                    That its means
are what it means,
                    and no one
should ask more.
                    The tools incised it
intaglio
             on a whole century—
fused
        Style Galante into
the blood of a man—
                    to raise it
height and breadth,
                    and of which
one says singly:
                    Music.

                    2

        ANDANTE GRAZIOSO

    After four days of rain,
                    the sun
    hesitantly
                above the film
                    edge
    of a cloud.

Brush it away,
as if a cobweb caught the eye,
the light motes of pollen
                    in soft air
pick up the dampness
                    and fall.
Tentative—
            a narcissus
    in the dooryard.

                3

TEMPO DI MENUETTO

Complete
            the light—
chance is not random
nor co-
            incidental.
"There was a man who lived
        in our town—"
Oh the measure
the
        complete
the light.

                4

PRESTO ASSAI

Because of particular bent
- the associations -
I could say that this
made music
                homoeopathic
music
        as I heard it.
The G minor darkness
cured me
        - thoroughly—

thus as like cures like.
That the substance was the music,
that it made of music
what the music meant.

§

Dear Diary
Wrote a letter I didn't like
to write
to a friend I do
like, but can't reach these days—
possibly because I do not understand
his connection with politics,
as, certainly, he doesn't feel mine
with medical research.
Later,
Köchel Verzeichnis 174,
which will be
connected
always
(schematically—
no Hollywood program)
with that research.
Hofrath Dr. Samuel Hahnemann
in Köthen and Paris,
Drs. Hering and Raue in Philadelphia.
Still later:
Slept the silence of love with my wife.
Talked about a sore muscle.
Thought:
Lachesis [65] might help.
(The establishment
take note.)
Then stood in a black raincoat
by the alder swamp
watching
the first blackbirds,
notating, mentally,

their sharp metallic
        calls
               against the soft wet air
of coming thaw.
        Returned.
             Ate mackerel.
Opus III.
       "Faber, is what I see in the arbor
one or two lights?"
           "One," I answered,
"it is Carl with one lighted candle."
"Ah," he said,
"when old people begin to see double,
then it is time for them to prepare for departure.
I am ready.
God's will be done."

§

Well,
      I've had my drink
(of tea)
        the way other men
might have a beer
          probably
for the same reasons.
            I've set
the pork bones
        (a little fat)
beans,
     bean thread,
kombu,
     (I like that—
kelp with the salt still
          in it)
onions,
     a few spices,
in a large pot

to mull all night.
Tomorrow
I won't need to cook
anything,
I can read
(probably some poems,
an old
homoeopathic text
with comments
in my second notebook.)
Letters.
I have so many to write,
and, damn it,
no heart for them.
So, after
a stab at the books,
I'll fill
up spaces
the way you said I would.
(Along with the triple drive.)
Nothing else to do.
I'll eat some of the bean
stew,
go out,
pick up an armload
of wet wood,
drink more tea—
the good black
I bought
from Wah Mei's
trading company—
or change off for a cup
of mate.
(Ilex is good
for my depression.)
I wish my head
weren't so screwed up,
wish I didn't measure
the days
in pipes, cups of tea,

                              and telephone calls.
(I have a preface to write.)
Yes.
        Köchel numbers
and more Mozart.
                    What did
Carroll Dunham say
                    about drug provings?
Someday I'll order
                all this research.
In the meantime,
                    another cup of tea—
light my pipe—
                oh—
                        hell—

IN THE KEEPER'S HOUSE

                §

        Each time
        the flash
        (every six seconds)
        strikes my face,
        it is:
        moon-madness
        given me.
        Full moon
        regardless of phase.
        (On a clear evening,
        the Pemaquid Light
        can be seen
        fourteen miles at sea.)

§

as moving
out
i keep
the sense
i take
i move
in short
impression
wave
        for
wave
        and to(o)

§

to weed out
or to put in
weed of the foot
planted
where no foot
was
climbing rock

§

—and there it hangs,
an unclean stir of
voices, echoes,
hammers, nails—
all that does and
is done to:
There it hangs—
the inconclusive

action—and the actors
caught between.
It hangs a shadow.

§

Run with the tide—
whatever it is,
                    wherever
it runs.
            Its movement carries
in and out of sleep.
        Run there in darkness:
with/against the tide.

§ THE BELL WEATHER

Not intentional—
except as it leads
with its lip
jutted from the rock—
what used to sound in fog.
Now, nothing more than:
"Cast by Henry Hooper
& Company.
Boston, 1848."

§

When gulls
            and ducks
ride it out—
swell of the last storm
preparing for the next—

moon rubbed against
cloud - the sun smudged,
a dying bonfire.
Sound.   Sound.   The ceaseless
sound pervading,
but low key.
Hiss of the coming tide.
I, too,
                    ride it
out.

§

Whatever it was I heard in my head,
I heard it—
                    and in that state
of half sleep it made sense—
perfect in some ways,
pluperfect in others.
There was concern for her
blue paints,
                    and the piano leg
that somehow rose
out of a garden.
Oh, I've forgotten most of it,
but I heard plenty
on one fine afternoon.

§ THE IMPRESSION

At times it is I who am embraced.
Held down.
There is no escape.
(Does she want me?)
(Has he had me?)
At others, contemptuous,

I shrug it off.
(Why is she here?)
(Where did he go?)
I lay my ear to the ground
to hear their passing.
I fear the male thrust,
and the female acceptance,
but I take them in—
my almshouse,
and my treasury.

VIEWS

§ THE VIEW FROM OLSON'S

One small window must
                            catch
knowledge of the harbor
                            above
a sunflower
            (in head—no bloom
as yet.)
            A fence of lilacs
brick and sand
                the back roads
of all New England sea towns—
this one Gloucester—
                        no matter.
So the breeze that lets
                        light in.
The best of it:
            A small boy seriously
sawing boards.
            "I don't think
Mr. Olson's in."

§ THE VIEW FROM JOHNNY CAKE HILL

Sail lofts do
            small business now.
Old stone and brick fronts.
                        One
caved
    in
        fireplace.
                    She says
"Everything's in museums now."
And we ate stuffed quahaugs
on both sides of the street,
                        looking
seaward.
            Well, the fleet's in,
but it costs $1.00 per to see
a few old blubber pots and
blunt harpoons.

§ THE VIEW FROM SCREW AUGUR FALLS

    water
        which is our element
    comes down
                con
    stricted
            at the juncture
    of two roads
                a
    con
        fluence
    several workmen
                    setting up
    posts
        look
    neither
        up

nor down
        so long
as the fence
   runs/straight/

§ A VIEW OF THE LATE FLOOD

Came across this way.
                 The stream
broke
    through
tearing out a
            twenty foot
section of stone wall
              milling
down the road
             as an alternate
bed
    piled
          ice blocks
four deep
          cleared the snow
evenly
        from certain fields,
left others
         untouched.
Wreckage.
       Mud.
And the bright sun
               against one wedge
damming
        the low places.

§ THE VIEW FROM HEZEKIAH'S

There is something in it
—angry—
it is more than wind
that takes the breath away,
sailing
            towards north mountains
which break wave
                        on wave
against the prow of the ship.
Keel to truck it shivers,
as I,
        too,
shaking.
            A winter leaf
holds on one branch.

§ THE VIEW FROM THE FRONT STEPS

Feathers.
            A plume
this cloud
            in a cold sky
over snow.
            A red
shadow
            on blue.
The unprinted
                        hollows
deep in the
                        hillside
below
            stiff
poplars.

§ THE VIEW ON A WINTER ROAD SNOW — ICE

Lit as if
  traced
in deliberate
    pen strokes—
stiff.
   These are not pines
so bent
   nor these
maples.
   Only the willows
hold their own bending.
Still
  and on fire,
a forest in torment—
sad beauty
   these cobbled grasses
above the snow.
    Breaking,
the light is
   crushed.

§ THE SAME VIEW BY SUNLIGHT

Pain bright—
   ice stabs
the eyes—
   along the road
(slight breeze)
   the click
and shatter
   falling.
Days grow longer now—
    the grip
increases.
   Whiteness
    opens—

opens deep.
          The sharp edge
cuts
     as winter's own.

§ THE VIEW FROM THE WILLIAMSBURG BRIDGE

1896-1903:
          Leffert Lefferts Buck,
chief engineer,
         and this morning
in 1970.
       Hardly a view
in the usual sense—
          too much mist.
The outlines:
        Domino Sugar
in Brooklyn at 10:40 A.M.
            Con Edison stacks
the other side—
        river in February,
and a few tugs.
        None of it counts
for much—
       simply places my slow
walk.
     I think it is that pace,
       the sway of structure—
    and two green-bronze name plaques
at either end—
       about a mile apart.

§ THE VIEW FROM KITS HUMMOCK

The sea is less than
the back
      ground
of its swamps/
           /tides
of dry reed
      and grass
whisper/break
       below
the bank
      light sea.
The cold wind
       against
wires
    tuned
      slam
of last summer's
        screen door.
A row of cottages
      between
the cold swamp
       the cold water
front.

§ THE VIEW FROM SABBATHDAY LAKE

It is not my habit
to
stand praying
I
do not sense
an
interruption as a day
of rest.
Small things   One
stone

set in a common grave
yard.
This, I believe, is
common
in shared sense,
and I, too, walk common
ground.

§ THE VIEW TOWARDS ALLEN'S ISLAND

Shell-thin
   blue
the day sky covers it
only to enhance
    a sense
of distance,
    stance
of hill above
     promontory
shore
  as this is
some six miles to the east.
It is easy to wish
to be there,
    but the view
would change.
     Perhaps
it is better? here?

§ A VIEW TOWARDS THE ATLANTIC AT 25000 FEET

Accustomed to the roads—
ribbons
   cutting across—
one more.

                        It is the shore
line, the
                    dark shadow is
water
                beyond it.
The land seems less
substantial.
                    The wrinkled skin
of the sea
                    some large animal
to be stroked
                    with patience.

§ VIEW: GRAND FALLS

    Whatever the pull
                        down
    lying below me
                        the poise
    weight of it
                    passage
    and strength
                    it is balanced
    by certain cuts
                        beyond
    where it had fallen
                        worked
    and left
                    an open grave.

§ THE VIEW FROM WYMAN DAM

    Ascent—
                the steps
    under snow
                the wind

its weight in back of
the land mass
                    takes your breath
away
        sailing
with April snowshowers
a north lake
            burying
how many farms?
                    Well, the use of it
is not their use,
                and I am not
impressed by hydro-electricity.
When I come down
                    I'll bring
a new landscape.

§ THE VIEW FROM PEMAQUID POINT

Striae—
            the long, up
tilted
        strata of the land
flow down
            congealed tide
against flux
            more evident,
rock breaks,
            the manes of kelp
draw back
            edge down
into the sea
            beyond the sea.

§ THE VIEW FROM A BATHROOM WINDOW ON MOUNT DESERT

It will not depend
         upon where—
a place.
       I had not thought
of what to see—
a group of spruce trees on a slight hill,
a half mile above the shore—
this, in late March,
some remnants of snow
under dark growth.
              One black crowned
night heron
        perched on
one terminal spire
          stops my
attention,
     as if he had come
from places I have seen—
           all of them—
prepares to take off
from those I will never
see.

§ THE VIEW TOWARDS BLACK NUBBLE

The wind thins blood,
still,
     the sun is rich enough
for dozing under the trees.
A bed of herbs—
spearmint
     is it?
We do well to rest,
and better, to walk north.
(The road will freeze tonight.)

Tomorrow, the first snow.
I see
　　　only between the trees,
an opening.
　　　　　If some night
the air would clot!
　　　　　　　Now only
what travels in a
　　　　　vein
against the day.

§ VIEW: A CHURCH, NOW HAYBARN, IN OHIO

A commentary on our time—
the sharp
　　　　outline
truncated
　　　　steeple
against the sky.
The windows out
and tiers of hay
neatly stacked
　　　　　to
overflowing.

§ VIEW BEYOND MY BRIDGE

Look there
　　　　often
as I have looked
　　　　　these past
twenty years—
　　　　　see,
instead of the white falls,
white,
　　　　the dress of a woman
whom I have never met,

nor will I,
   unless something
other
   changes the sighting.

§ A SUDDEN VIEW

Hits me—
   knocks at
the breath—
   goes deep
somewhere inside
    as if
something were broken.
Won't do
   to say:
It strikes—
   more than that.
I forgot what it was—.

§ A VIEW OF THE FLYING HORSE

There *is* a light—
   not described,
perhaps not seen,
   but
easily defined by dark growth,
spruce,
   in the half hour
before darkness.
    At times,
hard-edged,
   clouds
rise in it—
   feathers
and wool—

                                    even
              the life below them.
                                      If I say it,
              now that I have seen Pegasus
              rampant
                              above a field
              in Lewiston,
                                 can anyone
              deny it?
                              I must say
              no more.

§ NIGHT VIEW—LAKE AUBURN—EARLY SPRING

              Lights at the far side
                                      punctuate
              a coast
                          line
              Those who live there
                                        separated
              from me:
                              An island,
              rotting ice,
                                  some clouds
              between us.
                                  Is that
              enough to change speech?
              I mean
                              would we notice
              it
                    in a common greeting?

§ NIGHT VIEW: CAHOON'S HOLLOW AND EAST

Went there swimming
on a hot night.
Walked casually
along the tide.
      A going out
kicked up
      "a rout of phos-
        phorous,"
then
    turned back
to the sea
      and from the sea
again,
     shut in
by hard, high,
       bluffs / / /

§ THE VIEW FROM MADAWASKA—NORTH

The wide-sky country
  left behind—
      it is
(maybe it is)
     in the shade
of those trees
      these hills
which are
    tentative.
Will we reach them?
Are they
    always
just ahead?

§ THE VIEW: WINTERVILLE TOWARDS FORT KENT

Came into this forest
                warily
almost casually
                a wall of dark growth
the thread-path
                ahead of me.
What I didn't know:
                The crest
of the hill—
                ahead and ahead.
The stretch of the land
                directionless.
Bouncing back
                like a rubber band—
just as I
            go down into it.

§ THE VIEW FROM AUDET

Crossing
            the mountains
and a wind,
            blue air
above darkness—
              the winter
forest.
        One church
spire
        caught between
the sun .
           and a
snow shower.

§ THE VIEW FROM TOWNSHIP: LETTER "D"

Height of the land—
the dark growth
superimposes
the hardwood ridges
further down.
An island smokes
in cold.
        Far off
the wisps of New Hampshire
shut in
        the horizon
under a sky
        threatening
snow.
        Silence.

§ A VIEW IN THE DANDELIONS

Full bloom—
miles of
        full bloom—
the eye
        revolts—
dances in such heat—
nothing else.
It is the eye
seeing the eye.

§ THE VIEW: LAC BAKER AND LAC LONG

The mountains are slate—
                enough
gravestones for a century
                of progress.

The sense of these
                    pinched valleys
under them—
                    depth of a time
washing through narrow places,
                                    silent
but on guard.

§ A VIEW ALONG THE NORTH PENOBSCOT

What I see first is
                    white water
breaking over and around
                    ledge—
The wall of trees constant
                    both sides of it.
What I pick up:
                    one handful
of fine
        flour
            sand.

§ THE VIEW AT THE FORKS OF THE SWIFT
    AND DEAD DIAMOND RIVERS

It is difficult to say
which is which.
Each lapses into bayous,
as
each goes over
                    the falls.
It is arbitrary—
                    a place
for dowsing
                    inter-acted—
a particular kind.

§ THE VIEW FROM OWLS HEAD

Not the sweeping
        horizon
one is supposed to get
under such circumstances.
The cliffs
    sheer
        drop
grey shingle
      of the beach.
Tides beginning to ebb—
soft mist
    the flattened
fog horn
    echoing
to another
      one
out of reach.

§ THE VIEW: FLOSSIE POWERS' FIELD

If I
   knew nothing
about it—
     that the Reach
and Bay
   lie close
at hand—
     I would know this:
A sea meadow
    and upland—
brown,
   thin boned
like a fisherman's arm
extended
   hauling in lines.
(The flash of sinuous fins
too.)

§ THE VIEW FROM DARK HOLLOW

The dimmed light
almost illegal
as if something
beyond me
were shaping—
battles or moonshine.
The history in
one fall afternoon.

§ THE VIEW FROM BLUE MOUNTAIN
(NEWBURG, PA.)

The hill as ramp—
    a cleft
or valley
   either side of
it stands sharp
    bristled
with mixed forest,
     hard and soft,
but no dark growth.
     Those
who live here
    do not go up
often—
   repelled and caught—
their lives (and farms)
     wedged.
But the hill lives free
and despite them.
I people it
   as I choose—
laugh—
  and look again.

§ THE VIEW FROM WHERE NO ONE'S AT

That should be
            an easy
one to talk about
since there are
no prior impressions
by which
            to compare notes.
It is
        and it isn't:
Because it's *this* field,
road or stream,
                        everyone passes
with eyes turned
                seeing
by other senses.

§ A VIEW THROUGH THE ROSE HEDGE

Items:
        myrtle
                    (blue and white)
cinnamon roses
rose of damascus
lily of the valley
Japanese iris—
ash, cherry and woodbine
strangling themselves
on the way to climax.

§ A VIEW: TOWARDS TUMBLEDOWN

Cliff face.
   Impressive
only as its sheer
     drop.
And not that high—
      each time
I lose it
   I am reminded
of those few trees
     between.

§ THE VIEW FROM OLD CITY

So long as I
fought through the
war
  was
    with
myself.
   I spun
on single wings
     down
like a maple key but
aimless
   aimless.
      What I felt
was empty—full
    of
emptiness.
   Now I
have come here again
—not back—
     I sense
the morning opened
      and
the reed bog

                              curv
          ing
                    under foliage.
          The maples are about
          to turn.
                         I hear my own wind
                    rising in
                              them.

§ VIEW OF A FLOWERING PLUM

          Not that it is
                         more than
          the tree flowering
                                   next to it,
          nor that its branches,
                                   broken in winter,
          compose well.
                         I doubt
          if it bears fruit;
                              but the recognition
          of it,
                    on another errand,
          makes a part
                         of the day.

§ THE VIEW UNDER MOUNT ABRAHAM

          That cloud,
                         shower of the cloud,
          hides a mountain
          peak
                    and the ridges
          leading to it
                              approach
          of wind

                    the fine
        spinning snow
                        collected
        in pockets there
                        fissure
        the rock
                and here
        it is bright
                    in the afternoon
        tilt of light
                    valley to valley.

§ THE VIEW: THE LANDSCAPE WEST OF KINEO

        A country in deep shade—
        the firs crowd and bristle—
        almost jostle one another
        in swamps collapsing
        from a winter's ice.
        Few signals—
        landmarks—
        or where would one go?
        The likeness stretches
        to mountains further south—
        the lake shore to the east.
        Roots strike here.
        From pollard to pollard
        is measure enough.

§ VIEW: WHERE IT WAS WASN'T

        An hour's craft—
        patience of men
        about necessary evil—
        cutting the tree

hanging over the house,
                           and
defensive:
"Well, a wind might bring it
down,
           mightn't it?"
The sick wrench,
crack of green fibres.
A space—
sky off toward the mountain.

§ THE VIEW FROM AGAMENTICUS

Nubbled
           and hunched
out of
           the forest.
(Only from the air
can we know
                as geese know,
how much forest
                remains.)
Warted
           against the sea.
A place for men
                "high up."

§ A VIEW FROM THE TOP OF MY HEAD

That:
           Here it begins,
and here it dies.
I can go anywhere—
visit a burial
                or
talk with the dead.

I do not know
          where I have been,
or where I'm going;
but I *know*,
        and I am
released in the knowing:
Here it
      begins
and
      here
it dies.

§ A VIEW TOWARDS INDIAN ISLAND

It is
     pristine
apparently
        across
the green bridge
on a cool day
        in spring.
The church:
        St. Anne's,
looks a part of it—
a toy village,
and a good place.
Crossing
      changes that.
The streets wind in agony,
and a scream
      of shame,
our shame,
      is everywhere.
I cannot go
      as a tourist.
Even the trees
      ask me,
"Why have you come?

What can you do for us?"
Wooden crosses
                set crooked
in the graveyard
                reject me.
I go back quickly,
but I cannot forget.
I am the stranger here,
and I live on stolen ground.

§ THE VIEW: ROME SCHOOLHOUSE

Shut in—
                it takes
19 years from
field to forest;
how long to break
the soul
                of a place?
Items left
                inside:
3 broken doors,
4 window frames,
parts of a melodeon.
A blackboard made
of wood
says,
        "I killed a teacher
in here."
                The foundation blocks
(granite)
are falling.
Frost heaves.
The chimney cracks
just above the roof,
overhung
                by a
large   white   ash .

§ THE VIEW AT PLOUGHSHARE ROCK

A chance that I saw it
that way
     in a field
on a hot afternoon—
          thunder shower
on the make.
     The light,
and that frost split
     helmed
in a way
     that no one else
may have noticed—
       or perhaps
that was the reason
they left it where it was.

§ THE VIEW AROUND NORTH LEEDS

One open barn—
crossroads—
post office—
     and a
number of small, private
graveyards.
     The dead
stay with the living,
much as cut corn stalks,
half-buried in
     turned
wet soil.

§ THE VIEW FROM THE INTERVALE

Consider
        what this might mean—
a night with clouds
        (full moon
                obsessed)
not dark
        and light
enough to see your face
        as it
changes.
        That:
here the whole relation,
  being as to being,
life to life
        might move
clear
        over
into/another/dimension/

§ A VIEW OF THE OPEN

Now that you mention it—
"you" being myself—
there are closed mornings
apparently—
            but they break open
to the eye
        set steady.
The prow goes through—
(never mind the wake)
by truck
        by keelson.

§ A VIEW OF THE SUSQUEHANNA SNOW SQUALLS

I am not easy
              travelling
across water
              by air—
this stream in
              particular.
The beginning of the
              south—
turbid with mud.

§ VIEW-SIGHTING: CHRISTMAS COVE

Late in the year—
the white rugosa:
one
three
four blossoms.
Light on tan sedimentary rock—
the islands offshore
with cormorants.

§ THE VIEW IN NOVEMBER: LONG LAKE

Clear
clear
clear
each wave
is the sound
              reaching
to senses
              beyond
the sensing—
              break
of the hills

```
                    the
        fall of a few
                    late leaves—
        locust—
                the high writhing
        branches
                    and no wind.
        clear
                clear
        clear.
```

New York: September 22, 1969
Naples, Maine: November 9, 1970

FEVER POEMS

Perhaps serious illness, lasting for a period of months, is an important time in any man's life, though we all attempt to avoid the possibility. If one survives such a time, with its days of hope and despair, the world is a different place—somehow much more personal—closer. These poems are from such times in my own life.

§

```
        What do I hear?
(so very still around me)
        What do I see?
(so dark)
        Where is the wind?
(only its passing shakes the trees)
        The sun?
(only reflection keeps the light)
        Do I feel the growing?
(prick of hay against my side)
```

Do I taste fruit?
(covering of seed and winter days)
My last summer?
(autumn for execution)[†]
The last of my words?
(only the stop of earth against my mouth)

§

What can I taste?
beyond myself ?
It is not blood,
                    nor tissue,
nor anything I know of mine.
But it *is* me.
It keeps me from other food.
I am sustained.

§

When I look up
                    I see
the bell is back.
Is it too late ?
If not
        too late to ring it?

[†] The traditional time for carrying out sentence among the ancient Chinese.

§

Will the dreams make whole
what is part
            of waking?
or are they someone else?
another place?
dimension off my wrist?
Where will I live?
There is care in each.

§

Heat—
            sun smothered behind dark,
or what lurks in my bones.
Stirs miasms—
                        mosquitoes
lazy
        but deadly.
Blood-letting
            heat.
In the night it clears :
One star after another.
Lips and grass
                        drink dew.

§

On days when sunlight
feels good,
expands the skin
shrivelled at night.
I can forget it
            almost.

The fear,
        nothing but a cloud
smaller than a man's hand
near the furthest horizon

§

Nights, sometimes the hardest,
I lie, looking through leaves,
the maple, shading the house.
Fractured light. The moon behind it,
broken, spill of reflection.
Loneliness. All that is possible.

§

Not to make much
—or light—
        of it.
On a summer morning
awake early.
Looking out at summer,
calm as oceans,
          bright—
soft wind.
        How much can I hold ?
In winter?
        the fires of summer?

§

As bees swarm in here—
news of the outside.
Flowers, then.

Rain enough,
and sun again.
What do I see in walls?
Feel in this?   or that?
(Bees gone again.)

§

Not—
How do you live?
                    but
how do you live through?
It didn't begin—
                    no end
in sight—or beyond
                    (so far as I can see)
coming through sun.

§

Denial running through like blood.
It is hard to tell arteries from veins.
Active or passive—which denies?
Both do.
          One at a time,
blooms rise and fall.
Seed time.
          Look and see to the living.

§

dream
the lips crack
fear
muscles knot
loosening
        early light
wind again
faint exhaustion
deep sleep

§

The bright morning comes!
has come between grey days.
I stand—a plant in the sun—
growing. Dormant pores
open.
    That I may sink
in rain tomorrow
            cannot
cloud me.
        The moment is sure.

§

That day
      walking.
Green, as if green
had never been;
eyes   -pale-
squinted against the sun.
Loose as a colt
stagger
      over the fields.

Cool water.
Not too much.
Summer.
          The seed breaks.

from LÄNDLER

§ THE FIRST HORSE PRAYER

Blood
history of the word
goes back to
"hross"
Icelandic
for the scalds
and makers of
sagas -
survives in
our pronunciation
(North New England)
                    as
"hoss."
What does not
come through:
The sacrificial eating
in those times
when blood
was smeared on arm rings
                    and
a man rode far
to carry out
his own blood sentence -
rode back with
weirgild
that his race
survive   .

The figure of a man
astride his horse
above a fjord
remains
our consciousness—
a heritage as
measured out
in blood.

§ I, TOO, CHIEF JOSEPH

I am tired of fighting—
blowing my breath
                    against
stars.
         They will not
be moved,
                 nor is the
attempt I make
a movement.
                    Pure conceit—
my will upraised
but no discomfort
                         to
anything except myself.
I talk of "soul" —
                    concepts
that are nowhere.
                    I am
tired of fighting,
                 and I tire
of these battles
                    no matter
what they concern.
They talk of "revolution"
forgetting that the same
spot
         on the same wheel

comes around again.
I hear them wondering
if they have broken faith
when they don't feel
anger or hatred
on a good morning.
And I hear the sound
of wind like mine—
blowing at the stars.
I think I would rather
stay on here
          than seek
that grandiose
             sussurus
known as
        "public
conscience."
        I am tired of
fighting.
        If my brother
needs my keeping,
            let him
come to me.

§

I said:
Do you understand?
what a poem is?
that the song is?
sometimes pedestrian
information
          carved
by the action
of time?
the wording of old deeds?
Of Mr. Henry Bearse,
Town Clerk?

is the savor?
the salt?
        drying?
the kelp like leather?
thongs? on
            Barney's Mistake?
Do you know that
the land was held down?
by the weight of the ice?
and these mountains
were rubbish?
left over by bulldozers?
planted later?
You find beauty in this—
(fitting in
          how
the voice deflects
the ordinary.
I can use that
in my poem.
You find the sense dull.
Well,
read it again,
or don't.
There are no poetics.
You asked me.
As, gentle, you go,
know this:
It is the wording
of a seed catalog
circa
      1910.

§ THE AMERICAN DREAM

I want
      nothing to do with it.
Your life is structured
on lies—

on the patented
mistakes of your grandfathers
(and mine)
on the mistakes
you still make
no matter
how loudly we curse you,
or boycott your product.
You are wise,
with an evil
wisdom - poison
you drop in our ears—
these "porches."
Your wars
will go on.
I see no end to them,
until you have bitten
your own guts,
and died
a dishonored death.
I am not
outside it—
let me be clear
in my telling;
but I detest you
from root to the branch
I must hold to.
I do not want
your life
or your background.
You have spoiled it
with waste—
the effluent crap
you pour everywhere.
Your heritage is mine—
I must take it,
allow it to rot
down.
Perhaps there are
seeds—

some left over,
some new,
            that will sprout,
and may bloom there.
Until then, I stand
                        away
and alone.
            I will not call
truce.

CARMINA

§ THE FIRST CANTICLE

Lifts,
            not to the sun—
a place away from the sun
into rain—
grey rising light.
Rise light
            into it.
Singing
            fortune—
woe of the day,
or joy.
            Heaviness
dispersed.
A well man rejoices.

II

For joy—
            the wind is light,
the day strikes deep.
There is an end to it—

no end in sight.
For joy,
       the way of stone
on stone—the tide
comes in again.
The exactness of a place
where nothing ends,
has no beginning.
The air—the skin and bone of earth—
warms up.
         A feather glint:
A touch:
       The wind is light—
for joy of it.

III

CHANT FOR THE MORNING'S SEVERAL

It never does.   It never does.
I do.   He and She.
They, in the high fields
above the wood,
all do.
It promises, but cannot keep
to promise.
Runs away,
         clear brook or sand.
It speaks of madness,
of the days gone past
this day.
It dreams,
       and does not.
Never does.

IV

When he thinks of songs,
what does he think?

Joy? Dancing?
                    Refreshment?
Or does he think
                    darkness?
Storms? A high cliff
                    from which
to let out unspeakable howls?
(wind howling too?)
His hair.
                    How's that fixed?
Or does he think?
An ordinary, sodden day—
a passable lunch.
Small rain.
                    Song
in the stir of it.

                    v

Of skimming:
                    The lark, linnet,
or what I know,
                    the swallow
above a once-cut field—
the neap growth,
                    no,
the last.
                    He skims.
is glad he does.
(Or I am.)

                    v i

As it is such sound,
or joy,
        it is
the depth of it—
of wounds and

                         scars of wounds.
A place for burial or burning—
Sheol—
              and the tomb—
the death and charnel houses:
Where they died—
those millions—
                         again—
these.
              It is singing
for the dead.
                         There are the dead.
These are their graves.
Rock is their sustenance.
And in every tree blazed for song
I hear that sound/
                         /must
sing this song.

              VII

How he sings,
or what he sings—
as I heard him,
what he said
and did not say:
"thankful for that
much"
"Give (me) something to sing,
and I'll sing
              (it),"
But it's all to sing,
and all alive.
It is the place of singing—
last cricket
              under
a patch of warm leaves.

VIII

Bundle of asters
weighted in the rain—
last asters
           last showers
before the snow.
I walk beyond them up a hill,
to sing,
           look back,
or blow such music
as my knuckles make
against the corner of the house.

IX

Is there blood?
I see no blood.
No, it is the dark
of inwardness,
the leaves stain color
leached in the earth.
Of blood or say
no instance
                rises
or is gone.
A pure-toned morning—
lost—
           is lost,
and nothing seen.
The hint of blood.

X

No wild birds here.
They sing!
And that is tame
as I am not.

Rough edges cut
to touch my hand,
or work in blood.
It is not wild or tame
to sing.
Sing out.
            What is your voice?
and I will live,
                yes, live,
as on to it—.

            X I

Hatchings and etchings
this song
            (of ice)
or as the ice dissolves.
The day that had it:
Dark with dark is
early,
        and there is no day
except one nearly
lost.
I see it,
getting up.
Hatchings - etchings
gathering.

            XII

As those leaves froze
metallic
            to the tree,
left there,
                a frieze in rain
for what breathed.
It was their time—
still is.

Now let us,
        listen:
The parched rattle of winter.
Very good!'
I make a singing, too.

XIII

for Ronald Johnson

The rust of rock,
                rust
on the rock,
                but as it rusts.
I quote/
        /misquote him
as I have known
these rocks to break
in shale—
                the winter frost
to take them out
in plate and headstone—
rust and core
                of iron,
oxidize
        old orders
of the earth.
I do believe this song—
do not believe it mine.

XIV

What I could hear
was sound enough—
the belling of the ridges
broke
         branched wind
over
         hardwood passages.
I heard,
         as one inspired
hears no more:
(the howl of something,
though it be as close
as owls or foxes,
breath or breathing
from a wife or child.

XV

Whine and sputter of the wood,
drawing in the lost breath
                              nor last
as drawn out.
Do I see it?
It has gone from me.
Make haste this morning
while the sun is up.
The afternoon may sing
another tune.

XVI

The song transposes:
For if the eye trans-
parent to its core reveals
itself - no more -
it is a blank.

                          a violence.
Snow has ebbed.
The tide
            is dust
seeped in
            dry wells
are dark in
                   deed.

            XVII

Some damnable thing:
As if suspended light on light,
in traffic, shifting gears,
and held again—
nervous suspension,
when the heart rebels,
and the stomach demands
more food than the body
will digest out properly.
To sing is an art
which is more than feeling
no pain,
orderly contraction from pain,
singing.
            Singing in on weightless dark.

            XVIII

Burst open, flower,
as many-rayed as
sunflower—
lion's teeth
(the name at last)
salsify and thistle.
Say this burst,
(or I with you.)

XIX

The sun, among these islands,
in the grass—
swale stretching east—
an opening eye inverted—
turned away.
The sun, in praise,
has no such knowledge
as its rays.

XX

Whatever the freedom is,
I do not know it.
                    Let it come
of things not free.
                    Senses hold
the vise of wide horizons,
prisons in more surely
than the cliff above may do.
Let me, singing,
climb this tree.

XXI

Kick the can
                and
climb the wall.
                    Make
fortune say its say
(I say)
            and
as I,
        will I,
(time on time
rehearse it)

sing this song
that kids may sing,
bare-armed and all.

XXII

THE PHARISEE'S SONG

I am **glad** I am not as other men.
It has nothing to do
with feeling better.
I am glad because I look
through horizons
when others talk of church bazaars.
(Baptism?   They still do it.)
I am glad to look full
into the sunset,
and not to set it down
as words—
as it always was,
for what words were intended.

XXIII

After a good night's rest,
this song
            to meet you.
(What? Who?
will you be today?
Perhaps a different place
or meeting come of it
than what I knew
in thinking that I knew you well.
The strength of it—
the unknown notes:
What? Who?
will you be today?

XXIV

Wind as a halo,
touching—
            touching what I am,
where else,
            the parting
of the wind
            and me.
sings among this hair,
those leaves—
            and
as they say:
"The wind's not here.
It's passing through."

XXV

What is reflected there?
One sense transferring others,
a high song,
            thin as wood
bared and angled
                  to
a constant wind.

XXVI

And when I woke up
it was morning,
and I was alive
in a different space
than where I had been,
dreaming;
almost, I could say,
a different skin.
The sun had not come
over the low ridges.

Early.
A morning in December,
clear and silent.

XXVII

What did they tell me?
(voices
            voices)
were they telling?
(voices?)
were they
            (voices)
even?
Were they?
                singing
voices—
            voices
of the first or last?

XXVIII

Laughter—
laughter in the voice that sings,
that sounds above the wind—
the cry of bird against the sea—
a cloud that carries up—
the mist,
            the darkness—-
soft
        comes soft.
The song?
            Half-forgotten,
words and runes.
Magic.
            Phosphorous,
the wake.
            Laughter.
Laughter **is** the voice that sings.

XXIX

Whoever
        hearing
captures voice
or
    tone
revives
        and rises
seeks and sings.
I hear it
        so
as well as wind
that carries
here/away
way
    here.
And
        sound
may dim
as
    well.

XXX

Face come
        as
the originals—
            notes
of order
        strike to sound.
In all these:
reed and reedstop,
timbrel's re
            verb
eration.
Echo sounds as echo
does not give.

The faces
                    quiet
        whis   per.

                    XXXI

This thunder which protects me
sound for sound
                    will hide that song
which weeps
                    a disowned blood,
as surely as the snow
which melts, warm days.
All song is not to hear,
or given for a pastime—
joy as witless as despair.
I move behind the rain
in wind and blaze.
Thunder follows.

                    XXXII

That morning when I woke,
with nothing left
                    to sing about,
she said,
        "Do you want to see him?
He will leave today."
I went through summer rain.
He saw me coming.
By his eyes,
            I knew he knew.
The song hung somewhere—
there,
        and in the summer rain.

XXXIII

Hammer, true to its own ring,
sound,
        or the sound below it:
Boards,
        the hollow resonance
roof down.
        Or steel.
Or ice.
        Whatever hammer strikes,
from which it strikes and rises.
Song, pure song of it,
let it be.
        Extend to hand
and arm above it.
Let such be.

XXXIV

Within its shape—
        character—
range—
        this song—
the instrument that makes it.
Only this one.
        The tone would fail,
if it were other.
How the frost snaps in these trees—
the earth sound of these birds
melting it.

XXXV

If it cannot speak
        individually,
it cannot speak.

XXXVI

Good that they sound
                    far—
far off—
        these birds
clustered in the road
                    below
the house.
            There is no other place
left them
        in the sun.
No place to go.
Their voices sound
                away—
beyond a north sun
flashing on ice.
                No heat.
No place to go.

XXXVII

More.
        More than so much more of it.
Lent or not,
            it is windsong,
and leaf,
            and snow,
and water.
Come outside to hear it.
Sound.
Sound.
Sound.

XXXVIII

A chanting joy—
                he who sings loudest—

chaffering the branch.
What could that mean to me?
Thief - Thief - ?
the old thinking?
Who thieves or steals?
Only as I stand here
(thinking, and cursing myself
for that)
            I say,
"welcome."
            He welcomes me.
Music.

                XXXIX
WIND DIRECTION: NNE 20-30 KNOTS

Closed in—
our fortunes with the storm—
a muffled sounding—
footfall—
            crack of a branch,
rotten.
            Holds no weight—
lulls as it sharpens—
cadence and coda.
Wind backs
                and
stars appear.

                XL

As of the sounds
                this future
wind and water
which combine
                in pulse
to hold the ground base—
swell
            and contours.
Build a point on point.

Impingement
        swing
                ing
over.

XLI

Day
     light or song?
Cold
     light before sunrise
comes through trees and snows
silent singing—
           the penumbra
above hard wood coals—
cold—
     cold but singing.

XLII

Of specifics:
           How the sound
is clearer—
      as air, this,
is cold—
      the metal sings—
is ice.
The water flows—
          soft edges—
fading sound—.

XLIII

Well enough,
        and
well enough I knew
my way in—

the sun and song
drawing a little way ahead.
Later, it was dark.
The sounds,
              and sounds of light,
died away.
                I called them back.
I could not follow.
Sound that seems one way
around.
          When I was lost,
pursued me later,
to the place I could not go.

XLIV

Voice, and quasi-voice.
How far up
may a man
              stand
to hear?
What **does** he hear?
I know.   I know
it's mine and
no one else'.
But I would know,
if sound is sensate—
knowing—.

XLV

Wood
          tuned
as sound
              tunes
it.
      Opening in air,
      Subsiding in ash.
The last tune.

XLVI

If one—can one—
scant another?
Sound of what another
makes—
        as it reaches
me—
       behind me—
wind chime brittle
in cold air.
If one can,
          one
scants
       no other.
Earth relaxes—
and the water flows.

XLVII

Of bitters,
        sweets,
and equal.
How it turns,
         or we
or they.
       How sound—
but sound is muffled
in the thinking.
Never ask,
the answer's there.
Whatever places
-you or me-
        is there.

XLVIII

Once
     as:
"the belling of the wet
upon the wet."
I thought that good.
Still do,
     if bells
will hold their tongues.

XLIX

String or blade
in the wind,
as the wind hones,
sharpens.
     "Hones",
as all its congeners,
night or day.
More, after dark:
the blade
     taut
as string—
swells and falls
will surely die.?

L

Play on—
     play on
what?
That broken tree
bent over—
rimed in snow—
a cherry.
Think of its carol,
or the wood:

Is the wood yet
green
        or dry?
Play on—
a nervous finger
on the bark.
The days grow warmer.

                LI

Whatever mercy—
mercy means.
The sound is more
than thinking.
Tracks—
the birds in snow,
thieving suet.

                LII

Do not - lost change -
imagine bargain—
or that sound alone may do it.
Festival, or death,
the same.
And as I put these things
away—
            then bring them back—
to me:
        I say:
He who has such ears,
let him use them.

July 14, 1974–January 28, 1975

THE FLARE OF BEGINNING IS IN NOVEMBER

1

The sea and the land together
praise and raise promise.
They do not direct it.
Islands float offshore
quiet as a drowse of bees,
waiting for the turn of the tide.

2

The hunched shadow
of the house
leans red
in morning sunlight.
The slant/smoke
at the same angle.

3

Kicking the dead leaves aside
-a stone-
            -blocked and dressed-
another fall—
                moss
mute testament.
Cold-hearted stone,
yet some way living.

4

As purely meant
as one gesture—
the faint click
of a final leaf
among the beeches.

5

Move them gently,
as the moon removes—
a clear space
in the clouds—
echo clouds
          and moon clouds
-still-
          to dream.
The last cicada
numbed,
          and nothing stirs
that flies or walks.
A night alone
for night—its own.

6

Bright is not
          all of it.
The light comes clear
and pale as broth.
The flame will touch—
then burn
          in itself—
no substance.
          Heat
some distance lower
than the farthest horizon—
far as the faint bell
sounding the outer reefs.

7

Veering toward
the work of the world,
the days come

pearl handled
                    (and cold)
as a well-oiled
                    pistol.

                    8

Crisp as shards,
the ice needles
click
        as tuning.
They fall
-shattered-
in a capful of wind.

                    9

All bitterness assuaged.
The nights
                    ringed in cold fire
can be forgotten
for this moment.
In the lee of the wind,
flies drowse,
and I will join them.

                    10

You do what you have
to do.
            Ways are
the means of extremity.
Feel the wind
                    at times,
and warm
            at fires.
Fingers numb with doing.

11

But there is smell of summer
-balm-
      comes sharper
-focused-
      as the resin
from a broken branch
warmed.
      A handful
for the ease
      of shorter days.

12

Now you hear it—
now you don't—
hammer stroke
      hammering
the nail in?
Woodpecker sounding
for frozen grubs.
      (You do.)
(You don't.)

13

If one raven brings
bad luck,
      two bring
augury of good.
Across a graying sky
a number
      soars.
And one man says:
"All is luck with them."

14

The steel point
         of the time
sharpens as it waits—
spar to reach the spot.
Time that hunches,
only to refine itself, and
pick up strength
         from ebb.
A steel point etching.

15

With cold already in the wood
that feels like water
-nothing damp-
         A chill
strikes in;
         malignant,
walks—
         a terror in the streets.
And in the fields,
         among the trees.
A brittle finger
         trails—
and snow lies in the
ashes of the cold.

16

Whose season is it?
breaking the design?
I look at swollen buds
outside this window
-briefly forming-
that they later blast
and fall.

17

Life drains away—
slough and chaff—
wrack for the tide
to catch spring flood
dispersed in sea blood—
lost there
                and returned—
source to source.

18

I move slowly—
a lizard in my scales
-iridescent-
                caught in full light.
Never mind it:
Sun or moon.

19

To breathe a little—
all time is in this time.
I saw it first
as if it held with
this bead of water—
dew on grass—
sere blade of it
bent to the ground
in curve.
                No. Ice.
It froze and does not warm.
And on bare ground
around these blades
the sweep of arcs.
And those are frozen,
                        too.

20

Something of the past
defined
            nostalgia—
want of something better.
In these woods,
the night walks,
rubbing branches—
breath of remembrance.
And in the clearing
-suddenly-
            a bonfire
from the moon.

21

Length of the respite—
bated breath.
Each day its darkness
over the north and east—
and will it?
            bring ?
winter?
Clears,
            and
bated breath.

22

But now,
            the times of dreaming —
what the dreaming means.
We see the image,
double in fresh ice.
Clear.
        (the night was still
that brought it.)

23

By touch,
to follow those
who have gone before.
Woods so silent,
muffled,
          even to the wind.
The fall of
certain dead wood
snapped.
Susurrus
          and memory.

24

It was a long time coming,
and a long time remains
to it and us;
we've come through seasons
of it—others are inside us.
Breast of winter.
          Drowsing there.

25

Sounds
          are
wool
          on
water
          water
frozen
          fall
and all.

26

Mountains that rise from the sea—
and hold
          forbidding—
split as the red sun
works its way above them:
Cataclysmic/
          soundless.

27

Grey
          as the dark
is not
          grey
is not day
               light
or
     impasse
that
          there is
little
          left
between
               the two
as light
          resumes
after the
               (later)
moon
          rise.

28

And breached the tide—
as ominous
the skirls of snow

(or sand)
all in the flare
of afterglow.
And here
      and here
(here is)

2 9

As there is a start,
      and none,
there is no end
      on either hand.
Midway,
    part of each,
is true beginning.

December 4, 1979–January 4, 1980

TWO GEESE

§

Actually
there are
so very few things
I'd like to
see happen
when one of them
does   it catches
my breath
before I can.
Just now a flight
of geese

went up river
low enough
to be counted
an even dozen
without straining
to look up
against the sun.
One of those things.

§

Whatever I hear from the high-flying
geese above me
—going north or south—   that sound
lowers the temperature,
cold as the isotherm they follow.
And the wedged formation
makes the prow to break ice
ahead, and closes the way behind.

SEPTEMBER'S BONFIRE

I

Fire steps
in firesteps.
They touch
who are the touched—
the last
essential falling of the leaves.
They rise again
in such surprise
as takes the day.
And from the daylight,

its level shadow,
-ash and smoke-
the haze that will obscure
from step to fire,
to fire
    step

2

And as a sacrifice
this self immolation:
After eight days in the fire
the heart will rise
as a blazing star,
cleansed and free
from cold and ash
to light fires
everywhere along the ridge
and hip
    of the mountains.
There will be light
in the darkness—
and no dark at all—
a spatter of blood and fire
to warm the coldest hour.
(but backside freezes
in its own shadow.

3

In a portion,
apotheosis.
The day rises
out of the sun,
its fogs subsumed
in heat.
They fuel the light.
I take myself
across the fires—

incandescent fields
that drowse deceptive.
Last honey from late blooming
is pure flame.
I lose the elements:
Air - Water - Earth.
They are new metals
melted and reformed.
The fruits in sacrifice.

4

Water glint and
fire glint—
the spark
and sparkling
of the new washed morning.
Water glow, and
fireglow,
the coal
and dreaming
of the old day rising
on the sickle moon,
to cut the darkness
as the night
returns to damp these places
which will not damp.
But ghosts walk
in the shadows
of the place of burning.

5

No backfire, it is
restless—
on the other side of the river,
is not my business,
nor an affair

that I must enter.
Yet I do,
watching smoke
billow and wreathe,
rise
intricate the
heading patterns
touching
and expanding.
I hear and see
nothing more.
The *more* is there.
I stand here.

6

Roots become fingers—
and all become flame—
to hold—
as the fire conserves.
It does not destroy.
Plunge in the marrow,
along the warm artery,
searing, yet quickening
the earth
for the fulness of time,
as the shadows grow
longer and denser—-
their periods come
greater.
Nor heat to arrive
in all fires.
They shine in decay,
a richness— .

7

Wherever slashings—
rain as jewels—
crystals—may fall
into the long bend
of cold grass,
wherever such
may be—leaching
colors to the earth,
there is the fire
-orchard to orchard-
-leaf to leaf-
dulling and brightening
as thickets open
and this.
The quickening
in frost, and out of it,
those fires,

        too.

8

Do not stand
too close to the heat
of it.
      Eye of the sun
is morning's fate.
We are taken aloft
on the winds
from the seas,
where the tides
are informed from the moon
-rise to it-
-fall to it-
silver as fire
borne on the breast
of the night that will follow.

There is much to consider
-pain and desire-
much to give flame to.

9

There are pressures
holding the fire in—
how within its shell
it glows,
        and leaves
all dark around it.
Only the heat seeps through.
It rises over
world and worlds.
It holds and places
day to night.
The *fit* of heat.
One hand, one man
to mark another
           man,
and seal the beam
between them—
bonding.

10

As one of us leans
against the darkness,
the other lights a match
and pierces through it,
one small hole
enough to find a way
           home.
That simple kindling
will bring warmth and fire
hesitant
      stronger

fading
out.
But of the light—
no matter for its size.
There is no faltering,
and we will lean
a long way towards it.

11

And perhaps for years
the fire gropes
underground
to rise at unexpected
pitch—
a small
volcano in the grass.
We do not know it
until it overtakes us,
places us
in fortune out of
manner:
that the moment
is no longer
simple.
And this last grip
upon the earth
is tread.

12

It takes no more
than one night—
the fatal one—
for frost to nourish flames.
A final firing.
Break the web,
and end the line.

It is one more place,
and we have passed
through/around it.
Dia /peri .
The morning light,
and level sun,
view smoking wrecks
of such as was,
and is not.
It was recent.
It is past.

13

Pierced to the bone,
as the bone itself
is sharp
        is the prick
of steel
        of the wind
as the cold
        is the fire
of it.
Wind brings the news,
and out of far places—
one remove from the sun.
Yet the fire walks
here
    as everywhere—
stubborn to the last soul,
glazing the eye
in dead ashes.

14

Great care
to be taken—
that the new lights
shine to the center.

Is that point
a point of light?
That the core
gives fire
is not the source
of more than fire.
We expect too much,
and out of it
         all of it
receive only
what is there.
Give sense,
and lose sense.
Name it nothing.

15

Jewel and ingot
from common source—
core and socket
of the fire—
that which contains
and takes away.
Nothing has opened—
nothing imprisoned.
Both perform
and reform—
times and seasons—
making and destroying.
Deleo:
I lay waste.
Each day the turn
of heat.
It goes no further
than return.

16

Twin beard
of the fire
        divided.
It doth rise,
as sounds and sights
and touch.
        As warm
as these,
        it makes
the kindle
        from the flat and dull.
Bright combing be rewarded,
and the narrow space
constricted for their heat.
Warm hand and shin.
Not long
before the fire stays
this one place
        for us.

17

Path for the sickle
        moon
-sharp to reap-
and to lay chaff
in waste for cold
        weather.
That frost may burnish and
surround the seed
-protect what cannot freeze.
That fire shall rise as
fire shall fall
against, and from the heart
still beating.
        Beat.
But now the rush

of airs
that fan the edge of
fire to free.

18

Upending
Uproarious
They have their say.
Each part
proclaims another,
in the presence,
and far past it.
Unbending
Imperious
It says in fever
what the last may say.
(Assay and fix
the molten whole of it.
Each time forfends,
and fire takes the ingot
-presses in the brand.
The smoke will follow
surely .

19

Glow, suffusing,
as a log lain
in the fire
keeps its shape
and heat as counsel
to itself.
Once struck
it falls into pieces—
strange and hard
-metallic-
Kindles in a fury

the last time.
In nostalgia
rises .
Scent and beyond scent.
The last
last time,
and may it last.

20

Lost
lost
scream
gulls
rise
in
that
cloud
before
storm
downriver
after
they
catch
fire
in
new
sunlight   .

21

If I see her walk
towards me
from the light,
but do another thing,
and time it
to that walk,
that it be done

before she enters,
then the fire
of intent
has counted
quite as much as any
set and warmed by.
Yet I do not know
a place where I may
plan such things.
They will happen, ever,
if they do.

22

Of these harsh days
-the latter-
that they tighten
and seize on.
We climb through them,
one window
after another.
There is no end
to the room.
And heats which blaze here
keep substance
nor lose perspective.
I would not comment
more than what is
spoken as enough
to keep them,
and in readiness
to salute the spark.

23

I know no further
reach
the place

of afterglow.
The smoke
reforms above
the embers.
It gives a signal
as the bell sound
on the sea—
a strident call
at tide
for shoals.
The dullness
of the fire
brightens.
Wanes.
Brightens— . — .

April 28–June 14, 1980

MARKINGS

I

Against the wall.
Place defining
-scale-
     the spot—
and here
     he fell.
Draw me one
fire/breathing/dragon.

2

The water
            rose suddenly
in the night.
            It washed
a message to the sea.

3

To atomize, and
drive away the parts,
leaves remnants drying
on the rocks.
Is not to mark,
although it has the look:
(there is no pattern)
Shape. But shape is other.
Where the man fell,
walking in harsh country,
only a blood smear.
It is a clue to being.
That is all it is.
I read no record.

4

Diminutives—that speech—.
To hold it in the hollow
of our mouths.
Aspeaking. Many tongues.
Before the actual appears.
He walks in the room—
tall and straight.

5

And what comes next
leaves *that* blow
open to discovery or choice.
Very little chosen,
                    I suppose.
Follow the age of pollen
in these rocks.

6

Occasionally—
                    and for the occasion
a crumb left over.
Intentional or unintentional
mementoes
                    freed from keeping.
Their scent hangs thick.

7

Good one way,
the wind blows clear.
My sweat dries.
The corn lies flattened
-switched around the field.
Wind too low:
                    Its mark.

8

Markings in the air—
a wakening breeze.
                    They make
no mention—
                    passing others—

-passed along-
　　　　　yet widen,
(circles)
　　　coming back and
back again.

9

Travelling—
　　　　the moon has passed
directly between these clouds
and where I lie—
the madness of its color
on my lips
-a mark- no heat
persistent,
　　　　long beyond that time,
it travels in the grey
of shadows,
　　　　　numbed and silent
to where I burn
from having known it.

10

Figures of men - erotic
or winged—
left running naked on
naked rock.
　　　　Each winter
the high water and the ice
grind them down a little more.
Well, they'll last as long as I do.

11

Wherever the sun lies
light is evident.
Where it is dark,
                    light was.
The heat of blood
or salt—the burning rocks
of silence.
            Where the sun lies
is now - did - is not.

12

Might I think or believe—
(in this place I might)
And
        walk across it
leaving print,
                its hesitance:
That what will lead
must follow
                until it knows the way.

13

And if I plan to leave
                    a mark
I leave so little
-mark that means a thing
as any—
less than a pisshole in the snow.

14

    Tide in/tide out
    as if that cycle

-bent on doing-
knew itself, absorbed
the seasons and created:
Doing/tearing down.
One mark that follows
on another.
What we faced/escaped
made
     W A S H .

       15

Each town, its river,
named, and fixed by name.
                   Ha!
The town becomes the mark—
a scar replenished
year by year. The
generations leave graffiti
in their ruins.
Places localized by names,
ephemeral.
Each town. Its river
debouches to the sea.

       16

But if the mark remains
a mark on stone or wood,
what of the air?
What is done
         there?
The mark is not always visible.
It is in the sound
that does not end in echo—
continues
       sounded.

17

Mark of the flesh
-its heat-
wherefore the heat given,
and no man able to reclaim it.
Mark in high wind,
passing the one way
of it.
            Turn outside.

18

An inward life:
Mark travels slowly
-surfaces.
A stain of blood
fades
            long after.

19

Capsized - as if with cloud
topheavy—
this sky changes, but does not.
Change is of another degree.
There is mark here. .
Where to put a sense of mark—
As to mark
            as is!

20

A floor plan has it—
stretched to a limit
which is beyond the possibility
(no thing like this realized.)

Still, the mark contains the mark.
What can be made of it.
Intuited.

21

Whatever paid for—
paid out—
a length of line
secured to post or buoy—
marked in what is fluid
-staying-
            not permanent.
Secure, and only secure
on place/time.

22

We come to a place,
and we have to stick there.
It is not the best place,
or, sometimes, any place at all.
But, to leave the mark,
we must not leave
before the mark is made.

23

Since I do not wear glasses
except to read,
I carry them in a shirt pocket.
The case above the pocket
has faded.
How many places?
many marked hours?

24

Opening out or in
to the sea—
does one find such a place?
Is it one or the other?
What are the marks of the sea?
beyond the tide—
                    wearing—
washed?

25

I would like to move into
my friend's room
-but not with my friend—
and not with his furniture—
baggage for me.
I would throw it out.
Only his room.
The sun and the sea
outside.
The marks of shadow
on the walls.

26

What do I forbid?
Who, on the way,
forbids with, or against me?
If it is placed before me,
does it leave anything
to pick up later?

27

Whoever is found
is only lost to himself.

The place for finding
in one/inward.
That much.

28

Gebrauch: The use,
and what is of use;
perhaps to be worn once
                              only,
but used.
It is of this that we make it.
The mark is the seal—
only the moment—
                              touching.

29

Blue flying—
how else to put it?
thinking blue?
That is the mark
made.
What it is to make another case.
Blue.

30

Obscenity, well-lived
and buttressed,
is still obscene,
for all that might be hidden.
It is the mark
-a stain upon the hand-.
It will not wash, nor rot
away.

31

Not a good month
-they never are-
once I begin to
think of them—
think *on* them.
Ash, which disintegrates
quickly,
once the sheet is
off the calendar,
and we've burned more wood.

32

There is nothing I know of myself
worth the notation;
of others, very little.
It is a mark of several
degrees, and
                no thing
itself.

33

Smudging across a page
-ash or sweat-
is not
     (necessarily)
a mark.

34

Came and compassed me-
-a wind around-
that was the moment.

Marked me.
Blazing wind
              completed.

35

No one remembers
beyond the snail
-his tracings-
but if these intersect
with earlier,
a forest may rise up—
separate trees
from snail or memory.

36

I've worked hard at knowing
In the dust, these filings
filtered and burned out, too.
The mark is ash.
A sign of penance.
(Will not do.)

37

The rain—
Its few drops
falling
dark on stone.
To gather into color,
one
mark leaches out.

38

The sea, always the sea,
restless in
put
        out
trees kelp combed
back again
                mark
on rock
            intended
shores
        a
float.

39

Mark or sting - a
first reaction
press and impress
fades   the scar

40

Geese, no, ducks,
in line, a thread
the wake behind them
does not die
from mimicry.

41

When will I walk there?
over the stone?
to see if my footstep
(print)
            erases blood?

42

No reasonings imply
a reasoned
            resting.
Rest is not the echo,
not the force
indented.

43

Now—who do I fear?
The sound of fear
leaves tread
            (and/or)
mark.

44

Monstrance and indulgence—
the words coined—
we did not coin them
from something older—
something left—
behind the word.
And it is there—
a long time there.
We found the mark.

45

Did you know, or notice,
this or that?
Why did you take yourself
such distance?
doing this or that?

and am I?
        was I?
like the line?
the plimsoll, left for lading?

46

then-does himself
against the doing in—
the blood and gristle—
thew and sinew
            set there
on the post
-against the post-
take measures,
            wisdom.
Who will line,
or make the line,
himself.

47

I am not pressed
so much for time
as seed—the pollen—
float of which pertains
and holds - always -
a way to override the mark—
and leave its own
to grow from.

TO COME HOME (TO)

§

A sound at night
-carousing-
at this winter distance
could be the brook
flowing under ice.

§

Whatever winter flow
there was,
the ashes of last summer
show through it.

§

all of this
         under
stitching
         open
and bare
to the winter
- few leaves -

§ END OF A MAINE WINTER

The same fire six months ago.

§

Thickened to mist—
a fog gone bleary
in its freezing hours—
ordinary,
          except that
nothing is—.
An old man steps
              carefully
on his way to work.

§

Sitting here, craggy and aloof
over the melted snow my boots drip,
I am only one man
thinking for thousands.

§

Clear morning
it is only air
that makes it
settle.

§ A RESPONSE FOR CID CORMAN

It is true
I did not choose to come,
nor do I wish to go;
but while I am here
I will make certain choices
contingent upon the staying.

§ A WALK WITH SMOKE

As if I had known nothing,
until this
            fell
into my eye
the tears started.

§

If the wind blows—
what then?
I feel it where I am—
not in any other place/
other wind.

§

So close.
I want to give you this
before the wind
blows it out
of my hand.

§

Honest measure?
Men have forgotten them.
Only the wind and the rain.

§

Many sins.
The worst against the self
is none at all.
We run that risk.

§

Darkness?
That was only
a pocket in my shirt.

§

Broken—
a dish in two halves
on the floor.
Small sounds in the night.

§

Being
            intransitive
as
      the poem is
and
        nothing else
the music
            played
by ear
        that gut
so good.

§

Flat steps—
flap of a child.
She comes downstairs
gentle and smiling.

§

Loosening,
          the way
is like a snood or brooch,
opening to begotten pleasures.

§

House gone—long ago.
Well cover
          rotting
into the well.

§

It is a silent move—
remove as best it can:
Snow slipping into the sun, and
away from the house.

§ SPRING FRESHET

There are two liquids
over
       lapping:
Wind and water.

§

Wherever there are lilacs
the men died out.

§

I take spring pleasure
in it - what -
ever buffet of the wind
it takes to please us.

§ A SHORT HISTORY OF PURIFICATION

Bitter is
black
      as
drink
      is
ritual
      "atque
in perpetuum"
is
      green leaf
before the wilt
sweetens
        it.

§

This wind—
a live thing tossing branches.
Who cares what it does
to itself?

§

Terra Incognita
between the open faces
of these autumn clouds.

§

Lengthen my days,
or shorten the world,
Oh, Procrustes.

§

That day pleased me,
and no mistake,
when a friend,
to whom I had sent my poem,
liked it enough to copy, and
send it back.
His hand this time.

§

Down the road and
looking through the branches
as if *they*   moved is
someone coming (?)

§ FAIRBURY, NEBRASKA

A Russian whistle
-chord of the added second-.
freight moving through town.
The wide sky is
                oblivion.
A cold wound prospers in
neglect.
            "They die. They
die—."

§ THE WAY DESIDERATUM

Goodbye, but not
goodbye again.
I do not leave you—
land behind me
in the land ahead.
I step the curve,
and curve enough
returns.

§ TICKET OFFICE

And in the line,
waiting for what

never gets done,
a sign:
            "Wait."
More accurate in Spanish:
"Espere acqui."

§

It *is* dis-
cursive—
song of a bird
against the wind's.

§

A season on time—
arriving
                this way or that.

§

No reason to accept it;
but snow in April,
as at any other time,
will accept *you*
into.

§ OF TRAVEL

The only way
to go elsewhere:
Stay.
Morning noon and night.

§

Travelling alone on my birthday—
these scattered snow flurries
the only gift.

§ MID-AMERICAN IDYLL

Spring rains print wrinkles
on these faceless towns.

§

To speak
is already beyond the fact:
Now and again
an event.

§ A THREAD AT THE HEART
OF THE MATTER AT HAND

So long as the river
runs clear,
it should have the right
to conserve
itself by running
underground,
now and again.

§

Reaching across the table to
touch the hand of one who
made a friendly gesture, the
only reassurance was in the
light of the candle which
went out.

§

Do not ask
for more than I
can give you.
What that may be
is
the other side of
the question.

§ FANFARE FOR THE COMMON MAN

The absence of an aftermath?
As likely as no antecedence.
They are clamoring for what is new,
as if contemporary roots were shorter
than a thousand years.

§

Severe as the early morning—
warmth—no current
moving.
Face of the traveller.

§ CLEAR SAILING

Immediate love
embraces the moon,
and is drowned.

§

To whom I gave a key
I lose the door.
Nor do I give an entrance:
He is cheated. I am duped.

§

Seen through,
and shot with color,
the day is never
primary:
                    Blue or yellow.
Green and grey
                        it
falls
        into.

§

Spell this heat
any
        way
you like
            in
shade
open

                    the
            silence
                        of
            an inner room.

                    §

            How slowly ashes
            stir
            before there is a fire.

§ CHAPTER ONE FROM A DOMESTIC NOVEL

            She was standing
            at the kitchen sink
            brushing her teeth
            in front of the open
            window.   And I
            came up and put my hand
            on her naked thigh,
            and she put hers on mine.
            It was a hot day,
            after all.

                    §

            What use in August?
            all this wind
            blowing into the air?

§

Shatter this flower
if you dare.
Some of yourself
is lost
          as well—
and not to be found
again.

§

Dense as the shade
of the woods,
this sound—
                    a falling tree.

§

A razor filed on iron.
Crow's nest
                    (or voice.)

§

Here with us,
now,
uptilt of the wind.
The land is with
these
few pigeons flying
home
          (again.)

§

Circling, the motion,
wing over wing
                    and
in a leaf
the leaves occur.

§

Imprint on this leaf—
this sheaf of them.
I touch them all
to bless myself.

§

Numbering the grey days,
I must number all.
(The light, too.)

§

The frost of the last flower—
not *in* it.
There must be water.
Ice.

Let me tell you, William,
if every man who hunts
would pray before the kill,
and in thanksgiving,
                         afterwards,
you'd be out of a job.

§

"It's the most beautiful day of the year."
Until tomorrow.

§

Sometimes,
            if a man walks carefully,
but loose enough
to swing into the wind,
he might get across
a certain lush field in haytime—
the beards of the grass
just high enough
                  to brush with his.

§

Whenever I
consider,
it's too late
to do—

which makes it
all right
either way.

§

As I prepare to go out,
would you say
I came from somewhere "in?"

MUSIC FOR SEVERAL OCCASIONS

§ A CHROMATIC FANTASY

Calling knoll to knoll—
as bird's flight   falling
call - the houses set there—
rarely valleys
                doomed to passing
at their peril.
                Drops
sheer off
                their clatter as they
dry.
Do they?
                Sounding   how much
can I take that place
to stand and look
a passing
                tone - flowers do that
calling
                bird to bird—
fragrance their flag
elements knoll to knoll.

Cluster
     point
          as blend
accidental call eventual
as corporate
          (corporeal)
bird in flight
no such turn as stands
fall/arise.
       Dense
aurora filament a part
of it
     passage
          call. '
Deep silence down
Dare I?
     down.
A simple comport
consort to
          change in concert—
chest of viols.
Weelkes knew that.
Do they dare?
         Pass.
Link as linkage
-ordinary grass—
the stem
       standard -'st'-
for want of better stop

Association frees-
          not free
form as breath/spirit.
Take breath '
Position all knoll to knoll
call houses   birds
sweep   flowers   grass
en passant   for sound
dense

    wood
knock knoll link
pressure in pressure
pressed to stay
          ligature—   '
Do they dare?
        of wrath
the day
      develops.
Only chasm
once chiasma.
No stop between.
Road runs infinite
only as conception.
Words anchor grounds. '
Clothed in fire
         end stop.
Call to call dissolved.
Disintegrate
the integer figures.
Step and stop - purveyed -
beyond stop
step   '

    .

       Knoll to knoll
call to call
from call and knoll—
houses and birds—
birds dizzying place
apt to be
        at home—
at darkness.
        At light
a wilderness in
tempo   light
        well marked.
Washed.
      Make place

clothed in fire
        anew.   '
Era as things are.
Things of the era.
As the count
        (cast) of
call to call—
salute and need
house to house.
The birds fly through.
Made of such means—
a taking in concert.
Conserve the best of it. '
The chest of viols.
A clatter clanging
drops
      vibrate
the vibrant.
As tide changes—
forward
      deep   sustaining   tones
on rock
      and under
rock
      reverberant.
Assuage the sound
assuages
        salvages—
as those far ledges
at the harbor's
         entrance. '
Over the barrier
        once
and drops back
        ever
returns.
Knoll to knoll
rising
      islands
in the tide of fog

impressed
      referred
           below
the mists of night.
And this mystique
no clearer.
Let that go
in toll to preface
call to call.   '
Chiasma — edges
are sharp—
        the chasm.
Break from darkness
again
    here and binding
above - full square -
This fog.
The passing tone
develops
    layers
drop
   full space
as above.   '
    .

Knoll to knoll
call house
    bird
call
there is no direction
call fits form
it fills.
Breaks station
states
   no more
in limbo.
Breaks station
states
   no more
in limbo.

Breaks touched
break(s) out.
Call of the dish—
broken—
        the bones
shards
      marrow
in the wind—
the knolls
      dawn
the birds.
Ah! they will
a long portion. '
Not for this
        wearied
worn well -
wallet at the
midpoint—
refresh to return
wall to wall—
knoll to house—
to call to bird
as flight fall
dying lees—
to lee
    or leeward
the loess
in lieu of
what may have been
call or knoll
to bird
     house—
enhouseled
      above
below -
     become
the swamps below.
Whatever found does
abound in motion—
motive

emotion
the still ponds through   ’

Premise
        to promise
call knoll to house
within
        with
outward
        take bird
as wing for call
as fleeting
        fled as
becomes
        across
chasm
    .

Wintered it
snow on snow
the knolls
between them all . 8va
As houses
the air among
a puncture
punctum contra punctum
no birds there.
Creatured
        a character
sharp in seasons
to break -
break light or dark
knoll to knoll
bird to house
to knoll to bird—
stress as strength
the stretti   ’
    .

Curious distance
knoll to knoll
to house to house
and bird to bird—
hand, handsell—
enhouselled
break of the old
eld wind
            eftsoon.   ’
Verbiage enclosed—
released
to the prose of walk
among
            and through

            .

Taken care of
in such things
-sill to ridge-
becomes the silt
and down forced
impotence
            unlikely
a mould of worms
a nurturing.
We have that temptation
calling   knoll to knoll.   ’
Abreast of times
belongs resultant
such a time
            release
volare!
Strung near the edge
to return to it
-a feat of skill-
strength remains within it.
Herded - the
            woods—and
tree to tree
            knell to knell

a sounding.
Take air.
Whatever words are worded,
bead and rivet
to employ impair
bird and bird
the songs of houses
that knoll and bird
hold within employ.
                    (Knell.)   '
Call shatters.
Break time in time
insistence
            awash
the nights of seafog—
smoke to return it.
Awash again,
knolls as knolls
as birds
            the farers.
Flash of light
in pharos above tide—
storm returned.
One at a time,
and braid the threads.
Send as sent
the means
            recovered.
I do rise and make
that place
            of which I know
the darkening.
                    Call fog
and out of it
the brightness
            (strand)
cloud
      (strand)
the night
      (strand)

a tempting light,
as if the morning
were the evening
bell
    on bell
and cry
       ice on ice
as bird's flight falling,
the houses set there - call
rarely valleys always
doomed to their passing
Drops sheer off
knoll and house the passage.
Calling.

§ PASSACAGLIA

The law of ground:
"What moves the least, moves most."

I

And will come   well come
nodding in
make   make of music
Oh, that ear I sound.
will come well and
and as
       nodding in
sound   sounding
within round(s)
will come.
       It made
of image mate to
come will
       when as
well.
     Can swell

oh, canso
-los cantares-
is no babbling brook
well on the tide
removes the wave.

11

Falls too quickly-speech
as speech
            spoken to
being   speculative   voice
vocation   locus
transparent   local is
                as branch
permitted
            permutative
messenger who comes
angel.
        You, who take it seriously,
worry.
        Speech is only sound.

111

Taken with what is lost—
slow chance I take
important tense—the place
we've been - or not -
(we will imply we have)
or taken in stance - as
the man from the north
or the west - the sailors beyond
any direction - proof of the fact
of the lost   what is lost
what are islands presumed
as a part not seen.

Even cold, when cold is coldest—
evening the strait as narrow is—
the link of frost combines in float.
Elation is the chance—the gambler—.
Aleator—he comes—comes soonest
wave on weave of cold—the lace—
this frost—this even cold—event—
and happens to transpire—the leaves
in mist - a very mist - I try -
tried out the marrow bone—
and hone and keen the wind
for cold as narrow chain the
link of it and tell:
come bead on bead.

Or who presumes to cry—
that cry of emptiness to sense,
oh let that sound of let im-
portance - way, I see
by light not of the sun
sun's making   cry the
slow still majesties against
a ground   take sky for crying
(crime?)
        (is there?)
No try - or trying field
this time is heir
airs presumptive.

Thing   created thing   stands
off from   each day
its thing   creator

as in one to one
not one is not created
stands no variance
far off it has a life
this living self is
of itself one thing outside
the parent grieves   lays down
the reins   the given law
outstripped of
make the wheel each day
is weal and well as woe.

                    VII

wove   weave   as woad
waxen   root Tyrhenean
imperial weft   clasp
make and makes made
of signature - the signed
cygnet   young swan   to seal
to send   to make
                    is new only
contained weight aware.
Weight?   What?   Are you doing?
All was here so ordered.
Order is implicit
                    (was)

                    VIII

Bienvenue   ben   well come
to take this spot   pivot
feel out   open care
as come in spring
wells up out of it.
Can swell as
                    swell
great diapason through
the sense as sense is.

I am   not to be   was.
Complaint and make free
out of which the bourne
no end
        withe bent
holding clutch
the life of water.

§ SLOW THEME
WITH NINE VARIATIONS

for Brad Morrow

THEME

Cut it down
to the stem,
or let it dwindle
to the pinch
that holds its waist.
Hourglass with trace
of sand along its measure,
in the just proportion
as it moves away—.
Deflects the cut.
Restores - it deepens
sound or color   deepens
as it moves
between and deepens.

VARIATION ONE

Pinch
        hold in
waist
        hussar
and wasp
to breathe

226

is to
　　instill
as steel
　　　to stellar
stelae
　　sand
that deepens.

VARIATION TWO

Down to the cut
of the stem
the trace—
along which many
move to take
a measure
out along
recast its sinew
thin enough
for all proportion
measure and more
to raise in color
drop in flare
stem moves
(hour not its substance)
too.

VARIATION THREE

Of glass to count
by just proportion
what deflects restores
of infinite persuasion
deep and deeper
cut as sharp
abrasive in its passage
measured

                    to reform
        or blow away
        no trace remains   .

This thinking's labyrinth,
fly-blown and with vinegar,
this passage where the thread is lost,
and no hand reaches to restrain
along its turns:
This moonlight hazard
star shine and echo frost,
on this, once more cut
to the dwindled stem.

Let it, or loose it,
inner, outer,
deepness between and
color, sound of color,
restore/return
this narrow waist,
traced cut—blood to staunch
in sand the wound:
Or glass to see by.

Nothing restored,
cut down
it lies diminished
as the stem
that narrows
to its gauge remains
important

                    parted
and returned
it cups and holds
a trace - our motion
in deep sand.

Diminished   pinch
dwindling   waist
a young girl   in a forest
clothed   in leaves
Ah! Daphne   echoes
holds   to purpose
still   pool
narrows   deep

"And turned away"
quote in other words,
between the deeps
the catch of the stem.
On such a place,
and such beginning,
anguish as august—
the first of it,
and flow of sand
for counting out.
Sometimes it goes within—
away.

Or to reverse
is so to rise.
A stem is likely,

juice and sap,
its root in sand—
its waist the air
complete   belongs
in hours traced
and seen,   the glass
a moving air
of such proportions
come to measure—
gift of fruit
                reverses

THEME

Cut it down
to the stem,
or let it dwindle
to the pinch
that holds its waist—
Hour glass with trace
of sand along its measure
is the just proportion
as it moves away—
deflects the cut.
Restores - it deepens
sound or color deepens,
as it moves
between and deepens.

March 27–April 3, 1983

§ RONDO

If this is music, let it
play a bit, this playing
on, as sounding onto,
captures sound, let sound
break this pattern,
be it as
the break
tone.
Schisma—
plays a bit
being onto
sounding play by let,
be letting music play
itself the tripping open
stop the sound of let, the being;—
tone . . .
        be.

If this be, let be
play a bit   the tripping
sound of music's capture.
Let the pattern be the break,
the schisma sounding onto
open - let the break.
Be letting sound of pattern—
pattern makes its sound
be tone, and, plays a bit.
If this is,
        music let it
play a bit
        this playing on as
sounding onto captures
sound let
sound break this pattern, be at it
as the break tone.
Schisma breaks a bit
being onto sounding,
play by let be

letting music play itself
the tripping open stop of sound
of let
    the being tone.

Be

As one sound
bridges playing,
play a bit
captures music,
break the tone as if
this is music   let
it play the sound it
captures
let being onto
sound be letting music
trip   stop.
Let is being, plays
itself.
    Be.

One, the schisma,
be the pattern - break -
in any pattern—
plays the tripping over.
Trip stop being onto.
If this
    is music
let it
    play a bit this
playing on as sounding onto
captures sound.
Let sound break
this pattern   be it
as the break
    tone schisma
breaks a bit being
onto sounding play
by let be letting music

play itself—
the tripping open
stop of sound of let
                        the being
tone be.

Capture this - is music -
let be play a bit
the sounding pattern
break the schisma,
be it tone—
be tripping
            over.
(If this is music.)
Played as sound
on pattern broken.
there's schisma,
let it be
tone
        be captured.
If this is.

Music, let it play a bit
this playing, on
as sounding onto captures
sound.
Let sound break the pattern,
be it as the break tone.
Schisma plays a bit,
being onto sounding
play by let be
letting music play itself—
the tripping open stop of
sound of let the being tone
be . . . .

Played it this way
playing sound and onto
nothing marked, be
marked the pattern

let return be tone
be toned
    and be
remove from one.
Be placed—
and mark return and place
be played along
this music's capture.
Pattern break—
an open stop
      an open sound
be sound be mark of music
placed and played.
        Then
this is music,
    let it
play a bit,
      this playing on
as sounding onto,
captures sound, let sound
break this pattern, be it
as the break tone
schisma
plays a bit   being onto
sounding
play by let
    be
letting music play
itself the tripping open
stop of sound
      of let—
the being.
Tone . . . .
    be

§ CHACONNE

Will we be here?
Is there a question (why)
of why.
Here or there is
more than
       being
question-
       asks
for answer-   will we?
Being is the question—
why
    (in answer)
the   as
       (more than sound)
we have - Will we.
No question.
         Have
cut or graft
seed
    as corn will come
not as we will it.
Plant
    and move away.
Will we, here,
be among
       is
a question—
nothing more to be
ask why
     is
more than
being is less
than question will.
We   (why)
in answer
        we
will.
the —

Sound cuts the graft.
The corn rises.
Motion   Frond
Move away.
                    Ask
why would we be
moved.
            Will to be—
take the place—
fracture no speech—
no wind
            makes cents
as from the rise
to reach
one sharp after another—
and fall
            flat.
so fix
        and fall
the intervention—
replace them
will we be replaced?
The moveable
                    here
or where some
else becomes the sound.
Ask why is more than
is less than being
the wealth is here
the sound of (why)
Here being question
(why) in answer
the cents as from
the rise is
to reach.

Corn rises grain
to grain
            to move away.
Touch at

tempt the interest
replaced
      will
(was)   sense
in the cents
will rise or fall
a current - motion
moves
     in on tide
is why we
will be here
      replaced
be
  question asked
is why
the flower is
      being
more than
      pitch may be
the corn in rising
will.
    The sound
cuts   graft.—
a sharpness.
No more than
less
    the title
lord thereto
for those still here—
or those to come.
You'd think
a better sense.
(cents in great circle)
Take back
as forward
the thrust—
corn lies dark
in soil
that any does appear.
Will we?

Be here?
graft to whatever
branch on branch
to bole.
Tense above
the current
air—that passage.
Motive.
Breath's sure
dependence on
replaced is here
-we intervene-
Presume ourselves.
Ask why is
use all - in
use—
take presence
be present.
It is but given
use to be
all high is seed
the lowly
                 dark
remembers.
Whence/where
the intervention.
Will we be here.
Know, as appeared,
be here
                 ever
replace
                 be
replaced
seed corn
in seed time.
Mention it out
utterance   the tide
is spent.
Ask   ask
why would we

move   be moved
the motive
monstrance
repairs simple
fee
        the feofdom.
Is the question—.

And when the grass
does wane and catch
the wind
            a time to cut
and drop.
Thrust corn and dark
makes light
to be
is strength of whom
how
        wherever.
less the lens
of question.
(Touch spot cash)
is cents
            or are—
the spot:
            cache.
Wherever movement
tied.
            Motive *is* the tide
belonging ribbon to ribbon
is the tear and stretch
out
        being
road off a sounding
as the plunge—
taste salt—
it is within us—
comes enhanced.

Sound and graft—
to hold the root—
to be ever
the place of root
to take
        whatever
taken is
where   - here
the far   offecho
place
       meant.
(footfall   only wind
no person
         present.)
Mark it
       portion
scribed in
limit of the corn.
Where we are
were to be
         promise
of the extra
          cents
proper to the sound.
Of the surface
plunge
       the new root
as feeling
absorbs
       the sand
each tide
-bleach between-
a thrust implies.
Pliant
      resumes
a shaping.
Grows the limit.
Is the present
of an history
well kept, will

we be here?
To stay within
the bound of feoffdom—
question here.
Open current
or follow down
the tide
resumed as such
enhanced
the wind of sea.
Of all winds
question - here.
Will we
sound the dark
the soil
and graft of sound
resumed
       as used?
Sound of corn—
as yes,
yes to the answer
not a question.

September 19–October 5, 1983

§ CONCERTO FOR SOLO VOICES AND CHORUS

What has moved us, moves most
in remembrance. Movement most remembers.
The substance thins and pales
and sharpens.
       It does not die
away.

What moves me   moves
most in remembrance.

I remember as
the substance
thins and pales to sharpness.
It does not die
away?
       Away it does not.

What moves
          moves most
away.

Moves most, the turn.
It has us
     moved—
moves most
        returning
moves
    implicit
as remembered
         draws
the substance.
Be that shadow.
        Corpus.
Was it something
other?
    passing
strange   remembered.
We were young.
  Our love
        the youngest part.

Her hair was bright.
It burnished in the sun.
A spring delight.

The sun shone full.

Her face alive in sun.

A chime
        delight and bright
remembers full
the fullness of her hair.
Her face in sun—
a chiming
            full remembers.

Her hair and face—
a cheek for each
in shadow
in the sun
            poised
at light
            at turn from light
what moves us most.

I do remember,
though her face is lost,
the light that moved me,
shower struck from shower
moved the sun
and my delight.

And my delight was
all remembering
shower on shower
struck from light—
a light the sun
remembers as he shines.

Remember him—the sun.
We will remember all
that strikes the shower
from the shower—
light from light—
her face and hair.
Nothing lost that so remembers
face and hair and shower.
A corpus all embodiment

of spring and love:
Her face and hair,
the weave within them.
Remember,
          as he shines,
the sun.

Radiant, this remembrance.
As I stand again in sun,
to *see* . the sun:
Her face within the light.

Deflects the light.
That is all the radiance
remembrance diffuses.
Remember where she stood.

The rains have come
across that place,
and we have walked there.

Our steps have mingled
and with hers have changed
the place,
          and from the place.

I still remember.
It is the place it was,
                    still.
Nothing will change it.
Still. That stillness
in the spring.
          Her face
in showers—
          bloom
of hair in sun,
blooms as her face,
a bright delight.

A grace
      of seeing.
Seeming grace—
as seemly as the blend.

All remembrance is a blend:
From face and light—
of hair and shower,
flowers
     full.
We have remembered.
      (pause)

2

It was morning,
        full,
bright flushed.
Haze broke - light
as tide that reached
the meadow and was gone.
She floated in the light
that followed
        still—
full sun bright flushed.
She moved only
as the light moved
from her
       and around her.
Showers of light,
       and brief,
a shower of rain.
But that was later.

Morning
    full
bright
    flushed

still
    tide
I remember it.

That flush of fullness
will remain.
It is the true remembrance—
the last drawn bow
of light.
       The bolt
of suddenness.
He will not remember *her*.
Nor *they* remember
anything but light or warmth.
Cold that vanishes.
There was a trembling
waver
      in the air.
A song,
      or almost a song.
I could not hear. It
came no closer.
What I saw
was sound grown mute,
or mute to some.
I hear it now.
The form is lost.

I called it—
calling other names.
None fitted.

We heard the song—
no song was lost.
We heard what was given us:
a song!
      or almost,
trembling, as the waves,
the air grown mute,
but mute beyond its song.

Delight in shower.
Delight in sun.
We saw it vanish.
Those who sing are taken
in their singing.
Some lose the gift
they give to others.

Still
  and drop
to rise
   still
along the mists,
beyond the meadows.
Her form
    and face
do rise
    to rise
again
   her grace.

Just as the trembling
wavering the wave
of air
   in pulse
the mist
    impulse,
I must have gone there,
to her.
    A place we walked
down
   and sat together.
We talked, and gathered
speech
   so close
we sat together.
It was a dream
that moved us,
and a dream that parted.
Of such things remembered:

Why?
     We shifted
as the mists
         and waters
part.

As questions come,
reality recedes.
The questions
         never
the right ones.
There was a trembling
waver
     in the air,
A song,
     or almost.
We who heard it
dreamed its passing.
We who heard it
have it still.

     (pause)

3

It moves me most,
         of all
it moves me
to remember this:
Take these things and
weave them,
         interplay
of this delight.
         Arise,
and rise again
         to shower
on shower of sun.
Of sun light.

And I, in shadow,
do remember.
In remembrance
nothing's lost.
The pain is short.

The sun makes clear.
Its light has swept and caught
these songs,
            and more than songs,
her hair in sunlight,
and her face.
I do not see its form,
and yet I do—
its formed remembrance.

Remembrance loses.
Nothing lost.
The pain is short.

I lost the gift
in giving song—
taken in the singing.
I will vanish.
To some,
            I have
vanished
            with the mist.

Dream
            and more
to dream again.
I dream
            now.
The dream
            goes back.
I am no dream—
this flesh.

To move together,
part in dream,
is real beyond
the limits—
their flesh in dream
                    remembered.
The past delights
are showers,
mist and wave
and trembling
                over
out of me.
The flesh becomes my flesh,
my hair, and face
are these
            are hers.
The dream is flesh,
and I am
            fleshed
with more than
what I brought to her.
She would not know me—
remember
                now
the voices
            or the dreams
in showers
            of sunlight,
spun from all our dreams
together.
            Echo voices.
Echo of the past.
Remembrance not remembered,
no longer lost.
I find her here!

As I am here
in part
            passed over
mist and sun and shadow.

I do believe
                    remember
what I was.

What moves us has removed,
is mist   the dream
of sun and shower,
dream of sun and face
and mist   her hair on fire
-her face-
                    the past remembering
dreams delight—
delight and grace
in shower and sun
remembers dream.
The spell of dream is all of it!
Delight!

December 14, 1983–March 21, 1984

§ BALDWIN HEAD

    Sea spent after storm
against beach   a beach of shingle
popplestone granite quartz and gneiss
against the washes chain of waves
in chains against beach   a beach
of shingle popplestone in chain of wave
embroidered chain of kelp   in or out
and in and out belongs against a tide
smoke and storm

        spent sea driving shingle
into trees fir and spruce   popplestone
quartz granite and gneiss against
the beach the shift of beach of
popplestone   quartz   granite   gneiss

in chains of kelp of shingle of popplestone
spent in sea after storm of wash
belongs in or out   tide belongs
against a beach of shingle of tide
granite quartz gneiss   of drift
in spin of spindrift   spume
of sea in kelp after storm
against fir and spruce of popplestone
wash spent spume against tide
against beach after storm against
          storm of drift shingle   and popplestone

a beach embroidered in kelp
in chain kelp chain of waves
belongs in or out tide in chain of wave
against waves against fir and spruce
belongs in beach popplestone shingle
granite quartz gneiss spent spindrift

          spume of beach embroidered
shingle and popplestone shift of
granite   quartz   gneiss
popplestone   fir and spruce
belongs in or out
tide of sea spume spindrift
beach   fir and spruce
belongs in tide spindrift
the shingle
of tide
embroidered

February 7, 1984
Lancaster, Pennsylvania

in fields of flowers   flower fields
fields of tansy   fields of asters   fields
of day lilies   fields on fields of
flowers   tansy asters day lilies
fields of lupine roses daisies
fields of coreopsis ringed with
trees   a woods of pine and spruce
of ash and maple   birches grey and
white and yellow   poplar locust
blackthorn slippery elm
    the fields on fields of flowers
of tansy   of asters   of day lilies
fields on fields of
lupine   of roses   of daisies   of fields
of flowers   flowers in woods
of pine and of spruce   of ash   of maple
of birches   grey birches   white birches
yellow birches   of flowers in fields
and in woods   of coreopsis
of fields   of ringed fields   of woods
ringed with flowers with flower fields
white flowers   yellow and white   reds
and purples and iris in fields colored
with trees   poplar and locust and
blackthorn and slippery elm
flowers of seasons of fields
of fields following   flowing with flowers
and trees following   ringed with the
ash and maple and pine
spruce and the birches
    surely the fields when in flower
flowing and following flowers
in tansy in asters in day lilies
in roses and daisies in
coreopsis in ring and in woods

surely the fields are in flower
and follow on one and another
surely the summer in flow
the summer in flower

§ SONG OF THE TEARS

Eyes blinded by tears
blinded by sand
weeping in loss   weeping in sadness
tears
        salt   sadness   smoke and loss
the congeners of weeping
weeping conjured up
spontaneous weeping
blind as joy in weeping
blinded eyes
smoke   and blur   and salt
a sadness   joy in sadness
joy in weeping
eyes that close and open
wet and blurred
edge of weeping   of day and night
eyes
blind
loss
sand
wind
joy
leap to limit   edges blurred
limit of the tears
a vale of tears
weeping
            eyes

§ A SONG IN BEING

unto a song   that song's silence
of which the way was born
upborne   stubborn summoning
suborning the song by false means
destroys the song   it will
destroy its silence   build from silence
sorrow and great praise unto and
out of the song   unto
great praise   great silence   great sorrow
of singing the song unto silence
stubborn summoning cancels false means
suborning subpoena of false news
cancels that song's silence
must be/will be silenced
cancelled   the song's silence
upborne born   the song to rise
the stubborn silence   sound of song
no false means   praise and sorrow
great   as means   unto the song
that song   a song among
summoning silence   stubborn air
air of song   song borne in air
up by means   sorrow   praise
glad   surprise the song
song entrapped enraptured
unto song the praise and sorrow
the silence as the song
of way   the way of song
upborne   no thing false
to suborn song   the way
the greatness   song to be
unto a song   that silence
song   the way was born
unto praise   unto silence

—*for Janet Rodney*

THE WEATHER WITHIN

In Memory   In Homage
George Oppen
1908–1984

Out of scale   the consciousness
brave instance of its life
flickers   constant   inconstant
make and brake   the engine
evident   by degrees
announces clearing
                              seasonal.

.   .   .

The given,
which has concerned us,
no longer strikes so deep.
Age is more adventurous:
That is its gift
to us, and from us.
We might almost wish
that it were not so.
Old age is poised —
rarely takes that last flight
above the peaks
that youth tried to scale
in vain.

.   .   .

That one
              within me
within you
asks a question
of weathers

those that cut
those that heal
nights for rest
before the dawning.

. . .

A picture from within   a
very simple picture —
not that simplicity
is always the answer.
It is necessary that some things
grow complicated and various,
although the roots are simple.
Beginnings are within us.
There, they had best be simple
figures in quick   sure   strokes.

. . .

What I recall
is not instant —
not *the* instant.
It was many years ago,
and I may not remember
all of it —
          but parts
that superimpose
between myself,
and this, which is a mirror
-not the self- the same.
Merely what I recognize
one face to another.

. . .

The air   how light it is
wind among trees   a gentle
sussurus   a word exact
as leaves   but air so light
the voices   of men and women
are like that   a sussurus
within   a remembrance
of weather   the light of winter
flaring abruptly   out
the heart beats on   in darkness.

. . .

Whenever   and sometimes
the few limits bounding
imagination which is only
free enough to mark
the design of its consciousness
a will.   I hear the voices.
What I hear grows to
clearing   what is not there
not understood.

. . .

Not disengaged   exactly
there are always connections
which keep me in touch
with others   they are tenuous
as those   filament threads
that spiders send out
one clear still day in summer
shimmering   and catching
finally   anchored   each one to its
proper web.

. . .

It is not that by talk
we have said more
or less than was intended.
We have said.
                From what we have
said   other things have been possible
or have happened where possibility
has flourished.   There is no good
or evil involved   as consciousness
what is within the talk
that sounded indication
is amoral and aloof
always to be treated with care
with respect for what may
may not be beyond us.

. . .

There is no story worth
the telling of a story
no thing we can know
more than the weight of water
that passes by   its depth
either a river   or the rain
driving in   on a storm
all wind that carries.

It is myself that rages
out of a fury   just and unjust.

. . .

How fortunate the man
who is just   I have never
met him   mixed with
degrees of shade   I will
allow the good to bring him closer.
Let me see him!

.   .   .

If the air grows stale
there is change in it.
I do not know how   or when
but as I breathe   I sense
the turn as surely as
the tide   that freshness
which opens chance
that change already present.

.   .   .

A small
reverberation
the word
a ghost
that will not conform
easily
to what we mean
it   as
an example
the axe will cut
the word will too
not on the page but
lifted
          up
to fall where it may

.   .   .

The twist of the voice
as if it would
twine the whole way
around these long bones
an ivy which might
flower   and
from the seed within —

protected by humus of the mind
from inner storms —
a twist   quick and light
I know   I know

.   .   .

A fire of small things
opens in the wind
there are spaces   hot
but without color or substance.

They point the way
within to where small things
were greater
                    -early-
before the fire swept them up.

.   .   .

To have arrived in mere number
hardly enough from which to make
or take heart   to have arrived
something known within —
more than that
not way or place
in saying.

.   .   .

Bare of sunlight   or barely sun
this   light which surrounds
what is not dark in itself
barely the glow   which it took
from the sun   a borrowing
prisoned in the vital parts
bare   yet shrouded
not echo   not reflection.

. . .

A place swept smooth   a place
where sand and wind have agreed
to keep no record   each time
a mark appears   wind or water
tide or storm   will erase it.
The mind is like that   for all its memories
it has agreed to none of ours
individual conditions   what it keeps
lies deep   an animism
collected from all of us
in all conditions   our sands swept smooth.

. . .

The need to see past   is of our making
finally   yet we have seen into
less often   a heedless passing
swallows what is to be found
spews it out again unfounded.
Needs. So many things needed
as many harmful   often the same
without looking inward we do not know
the choices   how to choose.

. . .

There is rightness
a standing up
rectitude
the integer of the life
integer vitae
we will not claim
all of it
that is settled
outside us
yet a conduct
a weather within.

．　．　．

New word　　new world
each time a board is shaped
not what its growth intended
I grant you　　possible
only a possibility　　one held
between something made
and something not.
An old man looking at his artifacts
this one made　　this other not made.

．　．　．

It will never be　　the mere
translucent sound　　that allows
us to move through　　what we
have never and cannot.
Spaces within the mind
are more open than we think
them.　　The sound will gather
space　　more than space
sound　　left over　　the light.

．　．　．

Emotions engaged　　a consciousness
that all has aged around us
we alone remain young
that is the only way of looking out
what we find there
only on the surface.
What is within does not age.
We know only our own part
of it.

. . .

What may be sung   well sung
may well be sung   it is
that pitiless singing   changes
as the bells insist their tones
again   the ringing in stages
many stages   one after another
ways in or out down corridors
long stopped with dust   the
velvet of neglect   done
well done   may well be done.

. . .

Voyage loneliness   unfinished
therefore lonely?   no way to
put it   other than the chance
words of loneliness   voyage
whatever the voyage may be
or wherever we looked
any of us
tending fires in the galleys
where we'd cook whatever food
would sustain us
through that loneliness.
A fire   even to cook   at sea
is hazardous business   but
necessary   and loneliness
            yes.

. . .

The smoke would remain   long
enough to blot out the sun   to
lay ash on the living   freeze
flesh to marrow   all
that rejoiced or sorrowed   life

taken as a simple commodity
snuffed out   in that instant   reduced
to the point of our thinking   thought
which is usual   no longer
a horror   that we starve out
the loves and remembrances   as if
they were no longer needed.

.   .   .

Wind rises as a gift   to spread
the tedious   the untidy
in patterns   so intricate   far
dispersed   that there is no longer
a need to dwell on these
incongruities which stalk us.
We are cleansed a moment
ready to move on   and away
from the wind which is momentary
unsteady   and gone before us.

.   .   .

Let it be small enough   to be evident
that infinite lesson   of *all* the world
surely its type   merely that
we can't take in this boundlessness
enthusiasm carries over   but
will not enter the mind
in any way equal to these small designs
of blood   and of water
such that we see them clear
impounded.

. . .

Like a shadow   but not
there is too much   not enough
a substance not a substance
that the mind   a conscious will
should presume   so much
so little possible   like
but not   like not   but
so the world surrounds us.

. . .

Not the symbol   we are in need
deep need of scene   not what stands
for it.   We are fed the importance
of metaphor   yet when it's exact
it is the scene itself   *exact*
no substitution.
                It applies
to that day we need to bring
an axe against the root of the tree.
We need not reach for synonyms.
The blade's the blade.
Sharpen it.

. . .

Lest any shadow touch the heart
the heart be troubled we would be wet
our feet in moonlight
where the hill and mist joined forces
seamed   a valley seemed there
and a lake   and memories
old stories told by campfires
in the smallest watches of the night.
We knew that much   we tried
to listen and be still   yet
shadows frighten   and the large concerns

which blot out memory
moonlight   the pleasures of the dark.

.   .   .

An outlaw wind   against our canon
set up to move ancient dust
what is never   what is always
done   those definitions of our
littleness   sometimes fear
a wind far out   come in
that does not know or love a given law.

.   .   .

I know of no reason   other
than my own   an explanation
reasonable   will not answer me.
It is the true limit.   I have reached it
from a part of myself   and I
return for little   to what another
tells me.
                Opening   the weather.
It was here I made a law
of measure   wholly of my own.
My reason does require me.
My answer and my full degree.

.   .   .

It is a lake   its
promontories deserted stations
along indented shores   the
hidden coves   lie silent
except for chance waves
rising from a breeze headon.
Rippling and marbling a few black

cones left over from the winter's
drop   a silent forest
above.   It is not unlike the nature
held within us   all is natural.
We cannot   in the end   deny
our nature   create a thing
which is not natural.

. . .

Our substance flowing   in ruined country
that part of the land that will not
hold a grave.   Ah   the dead imply rebirth
and the reborn   rejouissance.
It will inform   it will come from death
that
        dead   there is the chance to breathe.

. . .

The brand of learning   that it be lit
is enough   it will be passed on
though few will reach for it
recognize its fire among many flames
only one more faggot burning.
No   there is much more to be said
searing deep   as one
hand passes to another
that nothing stands in the way of it.

. . .

How did I know that water?
I assumed its presence   not
that I'd been touched or wet.
How?   did?   I?
All such words which account for

things until they need no saying.
That does/can happen.
Snapped shut   the tiny lens
that will not turn loose
the prisoner   never losing scale
a seizure.

.   .   .

The words themselves   older
it does not seem so   possible
that words which we rearrange
with no difficulty   should be that old
without an ability to deflect
our uses   yet in the largest sense
they do resist   and elude us.
They make it difficult just at the moment
when they seem defenseless.
In measure attempted
they will assume nobility
growing from the rubbish
of our thoughtless assault.
Oh   the words.
Words live lives of their own.

.   .   .

There is an age   a cover of sands
which preserves it   and within
it does not grow old.   Alas we
attempt to enter it.   We cannot.
Only to observe   to mourn our loss
which may not be loss at all.
We must live as we live
in our own   which is no time.
So fleet.   So fleeting.

. . .

"Arrival Point"
Unsure   untenable   points of entry
more reliable in the time of Bach.
Not simply the music   although
all is music   how do we separate
what carries   peradventure   all
we are   from what it carries?
We do not   for all attempts to avoid
the true things   nuggets   we are joined
to them by this music.
                    Sure.   Tenable.

. . .

Sounds and waters wither
elements cross and contain each other
as they age and carry over
each to each   less difference
they will diffuse again   salts
spread   and scattered.

. . .

The land may seem dead   behind us
out of scale   out of color
where the light has left it
because we are not there to see
the angle of light still left
to shine on the land   no
it is not dead   it is sleeping
alone   We do not understand it
thinking we have left   that
the only land is the one we inhabit
to which we came   immigrants
thinking the life was before us.

. . .

These small distances   that open song
a plain chant rendering
our vanities   a single line
explored unto its close   which
with an added voice   would strengthen
into cadence   but a single line
we must allow it all to end
without conviction   that there was
an ending   this/these small
distances   the opening of song
we try to guess them and
to share our pride
this little trickling melody is all we have.

. . .

We explain ourselves   not others
although we may think to hide
through attention drawn away.
It is a lesson learned   not easily
as most others not   only by the time
we will have no further need.

. . .

One island to another   yet
there is more than passage   islands
set so similarly   worlds
apart   stone teeth among
curling lips of wave   they
are the artifacts   distant and
distinct   one from another   it is
a voyage of discovery each
unique   so distant from the mainland
they recede and crumble still
their shapes and characters will last.

Among bones   teeth are like that   last
the longest.

.   .   .

The harvest good   they must be
speaking of death   that is the most
reliable.   Only a few stones
mark the most recent   but that
harvest enriches all that follows
and the stones themselves   within us
scatter and flake   in the soft
dark earth   our roots fresh
nurtured in our constant death.

.   .   .

To summon the power   shadow
will appear before the fact   we
must watch for it aware
that not all shadows prepare for
anything   not memorable
they do no more than brush
the passing of the light   yet
power does appear   and in
some instance   that same power
welling up alone   to summon shadow
long after the fact has vanished.

.   .   .

The mind in age ascends
hovers   cannot come down.
There is "nowhere to return."
The turns are silent wheeling   shadows
high above the landscape   all that
bewildered us   in scale

but so far off it does no good
to know that.   I suppose
it is the human condition   that its parts
come together only at that place
where the fit is powerless   a
design   perfect in its just   repose.

from CASE BOOK

§ PART SONGS

1

A skein of flowers   they will spread
as flowers falling   flowers rising
fall in rise   as wind
as flower skein spread   willing
as the following in wind   and wind
leave flown to fall   in skein
another   another in another field.

2

Sun as leaf   the leave taking
taking leaves   their pulse
up   over   a scansion
line to scan   as spirit
leaves that spirit   in sun
light   lives.

3

Spare as light   cloud stain
dapple light   stain the wall

as cloud moves   one speed
lighting another   spare
touch of season   cold in
cloud warmth   one day
spare the next   fore
cast   dapple cloud.

4

Water trembles   let the warmth begin
its rise   in scale
perform   as this preformed
reflection   many lights transpose
repeat   are not the same
they come   in other scale
as rich   for wonder as
the first   when water stirred
the wind's abandonment.

5

These may double   echo echo
light returned   echo as
mirror turning to   the double
echo echo   light the mirror
fade and strengthen   fade to double
echo   that illusion.

6

Bell repeat bell   sound
over sound   stroke and shadow
repeat   bell over bell
stroke   shadow
shadow bell   repeat stroke
over   sound   bell over bell
repeat   shadow.

7

Heave   a vast turn
in water   swells
oils itself   slick above
water close   closing
to wave   and broken
a vast   turn
heave   avast.

8

The edge of love   as life
loves to live   that edge
split off   spills
edged and darkened   lives
that love   a tarnish
loves   our lives.

9

I believe the page   the page
as written   writes
to itself   a number
of belief   recounts
the making   becomes
a thing   unknown to us
still   I believe it.

1 0

Only a small   smaller part
to fill   what was
the larger   to place
the image   a stone
atop   another.

11

One part   another part
opposite   to move
wind   from one side
another   apposite
wind   in part
veer   of the storm
is over   parted
part   and   part.

12

How I would   if I could
place one side   against another
to mark   the dust
as change   rises
but no, it   falls
that place   one side.

13

Ask me   I will answer
to forgive   the question
you asked   earlier
not now   now.

14

No one   returns
along the road   he came on
only   the sigh
of shadows   in the dust.

15

Now hear this   this to be heard
the sound actual   becomes this
heard   hear and now
is here now   the voice
living   spread
agreed upon   (hear now this).

16

Steel sound   as sound is steel
opens   sound opens
the wedge   what is sound
no steel   no sound.

17

So what   so dark
the light   turns dark
the motion   one hand
against   another
takes   gently.

18

Believe me!   only
as the   exclamation
rising   strident
crow   call
takes   flight
belief   me.

19

Die cast   hammered
metals   thinned
to breaking   lost
soft ground   in spring
casts   stirring.

20

Fortune smiles   at death
borrowed   one moment
recovers   the next
a raptured   silence.

21

Take me   love's command
released   returned
thrust   relieved
relived   no solace
taken   passed.

22

Rough ends   fitted
fuse   into roots
of ordering   to draw
water   metals
given   growth
this form   transient
will return   many times.

23

Slow step   appearing
slowed   slowing

mention   retreating
age   follows.

24

Color of day   midlight
changed from dark   to sun
in cloud   it pulses
over wind   the cutting
shapes   frozen roads.

25

Therefore open   the face
a small hill   to climb
across   the way
outward is   inward
to ask why   the secret.

26

Gently   sensing
to place   under cloud and
in lee   by island
the shadow   of summer
remembered   the moment
all year.

27

In lieu of wind   too sad for song
delight in crystal   silence
in lieu of light   resumes
its call   in lieu of dark
directed   and into air
this time   in lieu beginning.

Shatter and call   across
exult within   the cold
a high pitched   friendship
doubling   as if they
these echoes   were the friends
of all we knew   of all we know.

29

They have asked me   again and again
for something   a handhold
up and over   to stand
higher than   high
in the place   in the air
where I touched   among sounds
shapes   those things
never seen   here on earth
I have failed them   glad in the ground
itself.

30

Now and every day   unto our ends
believe this breath   that spreads
its life   among us
in praise prepared   it is the breath
that praises   we
who enter   go out.

31

Blessed as the sea   in motion
not to its waves   not wind
the power   remains
in clear tones   pooled
not to see   to bless.

32

Splinter of light   around us
remains   opening
the petals   unfold
expand   and shatter.

33

Pool of water   standing
seeps in and out   across
the fall of leaves   around it
dark steep   the elixir
life and death   this pool.

34

Quiet revolves   in the tick of a clock
not the time   arbitrary
it releases   into something
else   the actual
it dies   away.

35

Chink of the ice   in the ice
against pressure   it rises
a form   we release
in our thinking   how we see it
not the ice dark   inscrutable
murmur   flow.

36

Who knows what is known   alone
outside of fortune   stroke
a lightening   cloud
of witness   let it be.

37

What I didn't need   I need to say
this opening and that   the closing
all of it the sense   words
held to bone and muscle   so far.

38

In this parting   of the ways
the ways   themselves
easy to reach   parted
but cohesive   the sounds
are joined   a joy.

39

In this small space   a light
the shining   catches
tangled   in a skein
above us   and below
we will see   the others
those   we live with
and touch   their love
so brief   their love.

40

After these many years   a bit of music
what was common   is most rare
almost lost   within the air.

41

Asleep　　is not the dream
the dream　　asleep
not active　　dream and sleep
awake　　alive.

42

Well and thus　　and so
to bring　　beginning
and to bear　　witness
all that　　portion
simply　　to begin
toss out　　a stone
a ripple　　widening.

43

Dispersed　　alone
a shadow　　among fish
schooled　　and parted
one moves　　to join
again　　upstream.

44

I do not　　often
hear a crow　　the
field on　　iron of
his　　proper cry
yet　　I do now
I do　　hear it.

45

In quiet   mid-country
alone   to sit hearing
the voice   of the blood
loud   crashing
thunder   the voice
of life   lifegiving
itself.

46

There seems to be   in cold
no wind   it touches
like a knife   cuts deep
before it's known   and passes
away   to the east.

47

The spring   taut and clenched
I touch   with fear
its force   will strike
or vanish   as the warmth of
early   flowers.

48

I have found   whatever it was you had
neither one   can describe it
closed arc   the closed opening
ah yes   but yes.

49

Harvest of light   the light itself
the sea   harvest of sea
its rise   and fall
a season   tide and all.

50

for Keith

I hear your voice   against my own
our voice   the many voices
leading   as the voice leading
point on point   until they reach
the mesh   the meld
it is one voice   our voice
a tone   in timbre
never heard   before us.

51

I did that   that I didn't know
that way   and known
I did   that I
this faltering   I am known
for this   not that.

52

No   to what I've seen
the seeing   time
relaxes   flows across
a little space   and that was not
a time   intended.

53

The flow of all   that silence
ordering   the night
I see   no reason
to inform   to inform
more space   the darkness.

54

Doubled   over
the attempt   is
one thing   only.

55

In all that   I pick up
I do affirm   my love
for you   and sense
that bend   of travel
where we have been   will go on.

56

Last of them all   that songs may fall
their distances   call / recall
their sounds   resound
and all their ways   one way
the last   no last the call
again.

November 29, 1984–February 10, 1985
Finished at Las Cruces

§ MOTET

Conductus:

Clear as any morning   light
burnish me the arrows
that I may bend the bow
praise sun   sun's being
being light   arise
within the strength   that will
exult   oh my good friend
release   the charm   alight
aloft   that I may mark the fall
of arrow   mark its swift sear
the glowing air.

Chorus:

As any morning light may
burnish arrows   bending
that the praise may be
arise   that will   the light
of bending bow   the charm
aloft   the arrow light
its sear   may touch
my friend
                the glowing air.

Aria:

Banish bending
arrow   bow and fly
the sear of wind
my friend the air
the light   oh morning
find the praise   oh
banish   bending
arise   alight

aloft   and banish
to spread light
the morning   ('s) light
aloft   alight and bend
my friend
        and banish care
the glowing air.

Duo:

My friend   to bend
the bow
        the arrow
light of morning
is aloft
to banish   spread
the light
        aloft
the glowing
        searing air

To sear the air
with light
        the morning
that I mark the fall
of arrows blending
with the air
the sea and search
aloft   alight.

Conductus:

Wind takes fire
it kindles   any breeze
ah shadow   that which fires
dark and cold   the heat
strong measure
        mind

your fire takes
a breeze   a breath intaken
kindles fires
              cold and dark
ah   shadow   fire
heat   this   measure
living air.

Aria:

As any morning light may banish
wind takes fire   any breeze
it kindles from the glow
ah shadow   ash shadow
the heat   is   dark and cold
strong measure   bends the bow
the light of arrow
takes fire   praise sun
sun's being
              arise
aloft and alight
the breeze   a breath intaken
kindles
         it sears the living air
a charm that marks the fall
the burnish.

Chorus:

As any morning light may
burnish arrows
              (wind takes fire)
burnish me clear as morning light
that I may bend the bow
any breeze as shadow
              (shadow ash)
the heat is dark and cold
praise sun   sun's being

being light   arise
the light of arrow
                        (praise sun)
strong measure   bend the bow
                              and
wind take fire
                        (a breath intaken)
kindles   sears   the living air
a charm   the burnish
                        (banish dark)
Ah   the light of arrow
exult   oh my good friend
release   that I may mark the fall
a breath intaken.
                        Sear the glowing air.
ARISE   ARISE
ALOFT   ALIGHT
PRAISE   PRAISE   PRAISE

Inception: April 10, 1985
June 9–15, 1985

§ SONATA FOR A SEXTET

I

Just as the voices
                        lead one to another
just in parts
                        six lead
                              open to one
another one   just voice
                              leading
down the ice
                        to fire rise
in moves of one to another

rising   just part
                    six strands
the talking various
                    multiplied
in layers just as parts
to another   no longer
                              parted
        toned

To lead
        in force
enforced
            believed
led out
            this one
to remind
                as others
in remand
                return
as one
        or two
or many
                various
variants
            at variance
sweet surprise
pressure
            rises
ice to fall
                to fire
scales
            precarious
wall
        superior
lapses

Tested the link
resolved in pressure
to make cognate
however the wish

a wish   fortunate
no longer parted
                    for another
          toned
to lead
          in force
believed
          led out
enforced
               remind
this one remanded
as others
               return
as one
          or many
(two)
          various
at variance
                    toned
leading
sweet surprise
the link tested
resolved
               pressure
fortunate wisp
no longer parted
from another leading
Just as the voices   parts
six lead
               six part
from one to six
pressure
               rises
ice to fall
                    to fire
scales
          precarious
wall superior lapses
lapses

Percussive
                to remind
others in remand
to another no longer parted
just   in parts
the talking various
another one   just   voice
six strands
just layer of the parts
no longer parted
ice to fall to fire rise
toned

11

When in earth laid down remembrance
carries wrong
                do not remember it
the ease of death
                against this darkness
will approach the light
                forget my fate
no fate indeed the fire in rising
over this no wrong to sway
laid remembrance down in earth
remember it but not the dark
as light they will arise both sure
the freezing as the flame.

            The earth
laid down arises   may that darkness
be of earth   that memory turn fallow
harvest fate or then assume
the wrong to sway in season
earth laid down in remembrance
wound and wrong allay
                my fate
remembered canticle of fire
approach the light

                      my fate
the fate of light   the singe and sway
of wing laid deep   remembrance
earth to be my song
                          as ease of death
when earth inlaid arises
carries wrong away
no fate approach the light
as down in earth
                  both sure
the freezing as the flame
                          and do not then
remember earth
                  that ease
that dark
          the light of death
my fate in earth

                    III

        Oar in time
                    to the water
        drip
              cease
                        ship quiet
        drop to
              curl
        pool water
                    over
        oar
            surcease
        attempt
                fish out
        quiet ship
                    around
        reed
            stifling
        heat
            upward

                    294

fires of sun
      light
striking
      cool depth
plunge
    so
oarsman time
to water
      rise
deflect
      angle
to the water

Repeat repeat
oh sun in dubious
haste and heat
presume gentle
as the wind in passage
fleck of cloud
dark motion
light emotive
as the words
of tenderness "Delight me"

Lost
      oar in water
in time
      to the
drip
      cease
ship quiet
      drop to
curl
      once and
again
      and
        again
and
      again

pool water
        over
oar surcease
attempt
        fish out
quiet ship
        slip around
weed
     stifling heat
upward
       fires of sun
light striking
cool depth
        slip under
to water rise
         to the water
so oarsman   time
beat
     oar in time
oarsman   oarsman

    I V

Instep   instilled
what makes the fire for the day
of memory
        the downward ice
the rising fire
        turns
a part
     such *in*step
step on
      again
just as the voices lead
in force
      enforced
believed
     led out

this one
         to remind
as others to remand
various
         or many
toned
no longer parted
nor despised
the prize in step
instilled
         to find
a way of fire
for the day
                  proclaimed
the voices are of air
of downward
                  ice
of fire
         the rising
inflection   step
instilled
still clear
         sounding
precarious wall
                  in layers
to fall in
         ice
to fall again
                  as again
and again
                  in earth
laid down to fall
or free of fire
sorrow's light to rise
made of this time
a respite
                  slip the oars
an easy stance
                           or singe
of wing

              the spark's a prize
of that prizing
                    bring the coal
to voice
               the upward ringing
flame surrounded
percussive
break instilled the step
still voice of water
                         stilling
flame   ah
sweet surprise
loosing lose
ah meet the flame

Shift and to shade
take steps alone
or with those others
                         consort
step breaking
              shift
to singe
              wing feather
dropped
              such shade
of earth
              resembling
earth as shift
is nothing more than shade
just layer of the parts
no longer parted
ice to fall to fire rise
toned
         six strands
that do not pull apart
instep
         instilled
of fire
         rising
downward ice

the layered earth
a stillness
                    brightens
          sleeps
intoned

Inception: November 1986
April 29–30, 1987

LOVE AND SCIENCE

§ HER SIGNATURE HERSELF

LOVE SONG IN SILVER

My love's a cleft
cleft peach her lips
her sex a cleft
off center cleft
that I may enter her
or so I think to take
ripe fruit so cleft
yet as she is not owned
herself her cleft
a cleft her own
not mine unless she wills it so   .

My girl's a weave of many things   I
do not know the names of all the threads
or lap or warp which make for colors
several in delight   yet supple.
It is cloth that will not fade
the dye was fated not to bleach
or soak away.   Her heat has burned it in

and if I look to see more there than
what she shows me   I will find
a pleasure in each shadow
taking form for what is not
informed suggestion   is so woven.

NOW SHE SURVIVES ME

Not close not usual
not anything I know
of heightened senses
her sleeping such
that color shows her
parted lips return
to quiet
stillest air
of night   and this is
morning   one ray
touching alien
to stray beyond her.
I must rise and
go away.

Of all bare thoughts
is this ambiguous
I love my love   but
who's my love
I don't know *her* in loving
this one "love" but through them all.
Indeed I do love *you*
my love   and how I must.
You mare my stallion if you will
but *only* if you will   and
I'll not count on that.

Who this?   My girl is?
How do I?   Does anyone?

300

Desire more?   than this?
to know this?   Who this is?
or what the answer?   Is it?
Who my girl?   I know her grace?
How do I?   who she is?
depends on me?   my question?
Nor is answer more than these?
her breasts and arms
her thighs and cleft delight me
in their season   both of us
will leave them as that season chills.

The center wavers
so I think   it does not
love's a burden   how it
wavers   no I step aside
and see no loved one
many objects   love's a pest
it lights and stings   a
temporary insect   yet my
girl   the proper one
remains   a flame at times
and I'm the moth
so close I'm singed.
She'll laugh   well
let her   some of it
will soothe the very wound
she made.   The center's whole.

ON SPELLING LOVE

I hesitate to tell
this girl or any other that I love
love's spell   for if I do
she does return to me
a void   then love's a double
and a dupe   a love not meant
the same thing   and a word

301

divides us   as simple lust
in cleaving   thrust received
does not   I will not say I do
yet do   and if she does
the spent both strayed and spelled.

She asks no questions
if she's real   she
asks none   nor would I
do well to   press the point
herself against me
as I strain   it is mere flesh
to flesh companion
in such merging   as it's
possible agree   all is.
That she'd allow my kiss
to take unusual
completion too she would and
to my great surprise.
Well, that's no saying
if we do.   No questions
and no answers.
Do not ask.

She will not know me.
Many times she'll think
she does   nor I know her.
The flares of anger
stray around our bed   each sigh
may carry us a cutting edge.
We will not know until
the word has bled us
faint.   Still there is source   all
source renews the chance
is always equal   so
for now let's take it.

Maid's eye   as flower
yet the flower will not open.
She who holds it asks me
wait a bit   the curve of thorn
she asks for   wait and
skirt the petal   flower
yet the flower will not open
if it does no maid remains.

Which one shall say
I love   am loved?
And if she will
how will I know her
if she looks at me?
Of all the moments
periods   this loving
is the hardest part
to us. It does appear
as fact at times   but
timing is its element.
It is not often
we are able to
immerse ourselves and find it.

These symbols for her   how
I use them   make or break
her   she will feel that too.
The commonness of what
she is   is all required.
She's overturned by image.
Let it be in vulgar speech
such quickens heart enough.
I quicken in her bush.

Whenever blossoms   blossoms fade
wherever heat   the heat turns cold
as love is embers   dampened out

unless another season's fuel
brought to bear   is ash.
But to insist is force in winter
she will not want that
nor I   a fumbler in the freezing.

A whisper of her elegance
such sound as
turns around the corner
of a room
before or after
anyone is there
a whisper and
an elegance
I build myself.
I want her here and
she is not.

Of many questions never
answered   I return
to give the questions up and
she may take them
if she will   or laugh
that I am bothered
by them.   Love if anything
is practical.
Her wildest ecstasy is
common sense.

To herself she will not
admit what she
admits to me   if I
see in her delight
a mirror of my own
I must turn away from it.
I gave her nothing
but my pleasure   yet

it might have been
a mingling   that her heat and
waters flowed in mine.

Whatever we have shared
has been a single choice.
I do not know the sense
she brings to what we
both have seen   and if
in desperate attempt
to stay together either
says we think alike
I know it is a fiction.
We do not and
something not our own
has made the bind
a commonness   but
one we do not share.

She will   and yet she won't
to talk would be the best
of it   no   and yet she
has.   I've heard her
falling in and following
the water sounding
what's up is down is
will and won't.   I
catch her legs and hold
them   the distance here
is not in walking
will I?   yet I won't.

AS AN ARGUMENT

Whatever voice we used
what   ever longing in
despite of what was voiced

it was in tone   an accent
how could we receive
what voice was used   we
spaced it   what we
longing   used in spite.
She never asked
I never answered.

In certain lights are
tones of flesh   the colors
speak and ring   I know these
shapes   caress them
seeing how she lies
disports and laughs at me
for thinking   what she has
to show she gives through
certain senses   and if we will
we may   but what does she
find pleasing in my
shaping? certain lights and
tones of flesh?   Perhaps
we both have thought
it will not do   it does
release my waters
flow all senses fluid
what seems as what is not
yet what is certain light.

How cloudless her eyes
have been   I've seen deep
through them   far enough
to know what I've seen
is not a film   the distance
colored only by its
distance   yet she laughs.
Her eyes are laughter.
What she hides is clear enough
yet something mocking me.

Say on   she says   I'll listen
yet you will not hear my answer.

There is an anger
strikes me
permeable to
what is stone
my stone that crumbles
at her laughing.
Girl, why will you?
Man, I gave you
what I had.
And all the night
goes by us
through us
angry as the fire
flying but
the anger is our own
this hot and airless
room   we call it
summer.

AN ETERNAL EXODUS

Each time this girl and I
come into a new place
a land or time of life
it is a different
yet the same   place.
Everything is memory
yet it is new   to try
to move in comfort
and to open locks
which have made of us
familiars to ourselves.
We had wished it
other   simpler   yet
we are still ourselves.

All our delights
are sprinkled with
a spice   pepper
acrid to all senses.
Still it is good
to shed our clothes
and know this flesh
is white in any shadow
from the sun or moon
our delights by the oldest
forms informed.

Her seasons
and her colors
change
          they
are the mark
of her cover
as the varying hare.
It   is similar
and will she cower
knowing the bitter
cast
          to seasons
all my own?

So often have I thought to turn away from her
and yet I won't
to find another yet there would be same
a face   a voice   its timbre
yet the same
I won't.
What is familiar is not sameness   nor
a place to settle   merely that
I love her   merely that I chose
and still do choose to fight it out
our faults are various
difference will survive us
that we fit   so often joined.

We'd not do well to
try again
            (however
what she wills).

        The devil himself would
        try to take or make
        a truce   a debt
        which would be paid
        no honored truce.
        Yet the devil is
        only one more figment
        something she and I invented.
        In all of this I ask
        merely that I rise
        she will open to
        one more occasion.

        That fine wiring
        tense with jewels
        strung along its
        noble metals   gold and
        silver   that we burn
        to touch   our longing
        reaches one another
        one   the day for all
        its shining   is outside.
        Our bed is here.

        How many pressures
        brought to bear   we feel
        the short delights
        together   nor will we know them
        longer   what they are
        they were   a gentle
        stirring sound of what's
        beside us   time to turn

from this one thing
to many others   look across
her eyes or mine   forget
to touch what other
senses did and will
the lasting pleasures   so and
as we were.

June 16–July 10, 1989

§ SCIENCE
for Ivan Tolstoy–in homage

I

A dialect of thought
between the languages
what could make them local
figure   past which
those soundings move
and coalesce   and break apart
as simple courtesies
that end in disagreement
time after time   yet fade
a long way from source
may help myself
to share that small part
no larger than myself

2

Think of compassionate hunt
for what will satisfy
bone and blood   the tissue
rent and shared
think of species compassionate

with specie   what is exchanged
or bought   think of compassion
it is only the fellowship of kind
the good old boy   dog with dog
the pride of lions become
a cruelty unthinkable
we think

3

Cadence   not to close
not to fall   that ugliness
the structure   not decay
not unfinished   new
will say little not
already   the settled dust
has fallen only   until a wind
a temporary rain has placed it
winds rising dry   to move it
not fallen   wounds bleed
as if to leave a record
path to follow   do not
mean   nor leave the spill
of agony   disclose
a level sea   a shore's horizon

4

Nor do they see   sing not nor smile
in loosened scarf of wind around them
eye through ice   rime chiming brittle
high pitch wounded   salt of blood
let open vein to chill as winter's night
descends   full scale of cold
against them   leap again to
rasp and whine   a bitter chip
lost snow   in warmth reminder
let it be no torrent

will awaken tongue   see not
to put affairs aright
lest evil touch demean   now sing
of bitter rasp   see smile take shape

5

Disparate parts   not to disparage
part and source divined
seen barely   waking as in water
a love of all that lives   in water
entering a life   as surely is that love
fluid that leaves eyes wet   through which
thin light   a filtering past
parts unknown   in closeness given
stone on one shore   found a distance
one other   how could they   parts
disparate   linked   there is knowledge
in stones   cut from each other
foundered asunder   source
likely in water

6

Beatitude for each survival
sweetness across cut angle
that voices might assuage
a sting   or bitters   what is cup
or meat   might not   bit
inaccurate   fine tuned   heard
only distance   acts become
erratic   each non sequitur
yet follows   hampered lens
in distance   bring up
shortly   curling leaf fall
change our counting century
not this timing   what's awry
a certainty   be as it is
to bless is wound enough

7

Intensity increases   distance also
close by blunt edge   leaks fervor
seen is seen dependent   vantage
perch   one ledge easy
breath taken   scale again
upland vantage   sandwash gentle
drop off profound   no easy way down
loose rock falling at a step
below a pleasant swell   greyed
so gentle   cat's claw   only
to arrive
                a fixed intensity

8

Down turning   lonely   no cloud
not to finish   finite tenuous
elsewhere   down cloud falling
zenith's not in highest place
article impacted   flutter wing
change lonely   so cloud's
article reaped in light   a
change rung loosely cashed
chilled zone imparted
levels airs between
so long as down
                so long

9

Not to say stop   as stop's arhythmic
cannot find an end to end it
say of structured arc this note
in sweep or shadow's form
is yet another driven
by this notice order not

so simple as predicted
space between these sounds
once margined pattern
take at least beyond this
structure at least awry
change period   clear lagoon
among sure lengthening   and mists

10

Moon's edge   hardly cut in
tide of cloud's weather edge
might bleed at least to light
might light to air is schism
what's appropriate   no halves left over
and to play with   curve obsolete
an attempt   return to it   not quite
the forms between undreamed   they
are not governed   symmetry unspent
off corner   sickle edge another blade
worth wool cutting   flow absent water
among reach   enough for sighting

11

Not that this   dim root
mad number   alive   wants to
says nothing real   easy
not enough to speak   divides
mumbling   loses grasp
below   how much to ask to
one portion   to another
portion   I do   not know
that this exact state turns
to matter   as fact is
not this   not living
as night falls   the root uncut

314

12

Who wants to say   the end
of a weaving   ending a rope or chain
bounded by where we are
one end is that   a skein
is knotted   it is impossible
to sort it out   this number
incalculable   an ordering
help me to find it   to say
who wants the end   of a weaving
or of parallels   do not mingle
they are unknown   to boundaries
districts of wavering   they change at hazard
of no one alive   to say
ends they do not see   a
fullness   wherever possible

13

Sun struck   out of cloud no voice
our voicing fills   void call
water remains   suspended light
for rain struck one moment
dark day redeems   itself
only once struck   implies
sound belied   fear dawns
we blind in it   as only
cloud   a day behind great woods
a hair of branches hangs   my son
my son   that I had died
for what is greatness   out of cloud

The the this and then
thistle thrust thickness
absolute the   nothing tone

texture   tensed   oh wave
in willing   what will   woe
to this   that thrust   be able
threat be cunning   wherein
no good   no doom down
web wear this   the the
the down of thistle   stride
this margin   then in thickness
once broken   set   does not cohere
inherent coast   line this and then
thrust the the the
then tone   tense wave
wear   the the hearing

15

Look to them   my keys
no need to light   day light
lasts   eye into cold crystal
lest it lose   a key to mirror
against reflection   one enclosed
an airless room exact   it will not
as play no games   I'm closer
to it will not now   a space
look into how *he* did it   no
one did   it was   curve holding
line   at all dimensions keys
no longer mine   snow has buried them

16

Length of line   not loosing
where I go   any going
doppelganger   where've I seen
you   before   as doubles
not remembrance   form
familiar   not identical   wave
once prophesied   the look

not likeness   is exact
so of the things   untrue
expectance   nostalgia likely
I'd draw in   line comes
tautened   what is anchored
to another end of it

17

Of obeisance   clamor
we have descended into fire
forgotten sources of this heat
which rises leaving   perch
uncertainties   what was here
what gave us   we do not
do it so   no more
nor can we still repair
few remnants   holdouts left
and dying   in the cripple
of a pendulum   or spring
ignored   with nothing competent
to take its place   is not a generation
following   obsolescence of the living bone

18

Hands on stone   or other stones
to be left put   did not leave
where they were   an arrogance
to propose   or forecast   find
what is as is   not
hands on other left mark
arrogance   resurgent what
of forms not seen   the town
is not a mere topography
ordering more tempting space
void is no color   black
as true as white as
stone   color

19

Closing   opening wing
airless to air   reverberant
now it is isn't   as
heat rising   trembles cold
bears wind   another trend
same wind around   close
open lest the wing be shattered
hills turned salt   sting
poised against pain   as revenant
what is remembered   rising
not to wonder   nor to feel it
just ends to be what is honest
pay attention to the   wing
not wing   approaching

Thin as air   no estrangement
from the actual   what is
not comparison   how would you
put this in terms   we might
make use   it will not work
out   why the thin sphere
around us   girt in   what it
reaches   nothing sufficient
would not know   its breadth
length   as of days   agree
with water   shaft of sun
light to drink up nothing
but in the eye   beheld
an air   astringent   but
to sense

Stasis   what is
more   not to center
off   to fly
off to
        make
stasis   stand or
stanza
        to is
what   is not to
where   would be
left   glister   light flake
stay   staying   stain
what you make of it

To words   again let words
pour   be magic   of that coin
negotiable   as speech   that some
will waste   on rock
deserted ground   where pinch of dust
may settle   crevice nurtures
if storm arises   not to wash
to swell   break husk   but words
take root   a cognizance   to
touch   or will not be enough
explain to me   this rock
is enough within itself   the words
dry out as something not
their province   word or stone
these objects

Self's not to borrow   smother
place in gold   leaf thread

tapestry's awry   no garden
walled   nor unicorn   a rose
impaled   thorn's self
blood issue   stem that's hard to be
as music   notes aligned or piled
long bow   bar   broken into wave
wind wander   light's emotion
senses   let one be   not as mine
I talk for sense   to make it clear
I cannot   these are simple forms
I do not know them   other
as they move away   not mine

24

Whose meaning has depth   for us
a strangeness   limit what is strange
to what is ordinary   the light
which reaches this wall   may
ricochet   another's opposite
but not an echo   not reflection
it is suffused   this lighting
where depth   a coastal
occurrence   so girded as rock
or sand   a light between partitions
the chambers of the heart   in
closed rooms   also meaning
and a depth   dare strike a match
nor fall   far enough to shatter

25

About to hear   crusis/anacrusis
there might be   staying power
simple means   for touch
between terms   up   or
not to be   whatever it
did it   touch

simply hard   to prepare
pared down   enough
there is   one between
some   thing
listen   stopped

26

Unlikeness to what degree   what to know
what it is   it is not likely
things do   not explain themselves   as
other   they explain each   how to
touch a weakening   each
other likely   unlike anything
we know   not this stone   of
stone   undisturbed degree
I am not what I think I am
to one degree   lost in another
explain you   this stone   one distant
light   for want of better   call it star

27

What ever we cannot   call it ethics
call it   what is naming   I do not
have the tools   other than the words
words alive   and left to me
their singleness   their purpose
is their own proposed   whatever
can be   they contain a secret
I would not answer it answer to it
if I could   call it what I presume
it to be   the word goes elsewhere
rarely   exact to a mark   I think
I gauge by eye   my eye is
small enough to open it
tightening quoin   as press comes last

28

Possible as impossible   they seem
vacant as eye seen seeming
to tell one or another
scribes circle   and around
is only living
only magic   by attempt
nor scales of goodness
I would not follow such a trade
it has no parts   is not
coherent   what is good
remains subjective   subject
is its only subject

Glass into glass   a great hall
opening   it opens only to the open
eye occasional   the small hole
in   to one imagined mirror
endless if we see enough
another mirror   yet not there
glassed   one would gloss over
text   or test a ringing in another
out   I'd not found it earlier
now it is nothing but remembrance
that it is not sequence but entire
the system falters when it tries for us
says we do   preens and flatters
nothing but occasional   smoke

30

To look not find   things fit
how they move   in their splitting
show the fit of purpose
edge of continents   washed by opposite seas
androgynous   that in fit there is purpose

there is burgeon   there are things
we do not know   could never know
it is not in what we amass
that there is more than knowledge
mere beckoning   we think we know
we think the findings are our own
the seas   move   selfless
without emotion   swallow our screaming
we think we have lost them
nothing loses

31

Not one's position
                    not one's pleasure
not one's feeling
                    not for anything
not that there are principles
                              not   not
what one of us might say
                    what do
what ever
          every or the several
where we stand
                    where we might not

32

Into the look of the time   in
which I live   the look   of many
I do not know   more than my own
in one sense   one lens   I
bring to bear   but I do   know
what is hardly mine   I
remember   by a prompting
it is blood and privy to
what I cannot know   I
recognize this building   joins

into the air   I know
nothing of those who built it
except for join   the loosening
look of time   or any timing

33

Within a circle   any figure
presupposed   a circle   harboring
no magic   will ignore the fit
full falling as inside becalmed
there is   whatever will continues
I see no other   see no reason
reason being claim   within the circle
vanity is all that's wanted to imply
things framed outside   a sailing
will not leak   the hull is caulked
imply a reason   strike the shutter
crying confident   all's well within

34

Fallen from fires   as a heat must rise
it was not cold enough   bare floors in winter
our naked flesh to chill   as fires
what we think enclosed   no do not
try to hold it in   the bent is fury
weather swept   where or whether
the fall is not its fury
we have tried too hard   to touch
what we do not know   I want my moon
the young girl crying   drunken poet
from his boat   to dive   in fire
harken fire   around us   oh let us fall
evoke   know nothing   we are not sure of it

35

Music continues   before news
as absolute   of mathematics
do not leave it there   music
is its own transcendence
what do I know   I could give
anyone who asked   but let
them listen   what comes from us
is in this music   news   it is blood flow
what continues   yet that is not all
it has been   before we knew it
moving to a light   opens what we knew
before we knew we did not flow
continuing   a music

36

Back and back   plunged into its own death
wing of a bird   of a sound
which occurs   it is the possible
fall   or a failure to be
it is this and not this   back and
back   handed into a wave
as whirr of a wing   back
it is attempt   but not tempted
to know more   but to remain nothing
not to control   or be controlled
its own center eccentric
back and back   reaching the skill
of blood   it is this place
it is the furthest form
final   a call for familiars

37

Not ourselves   what is generated
out of generation   a convenience

to speak of it   measure time
if this is so   is that leading
to believe   we can know anything
enough   will set to it   the wall
will not breach   it is unlikely
we have moved it   wishing   it ends
a place   near a far gate
wailing for lost chance   so it is
thought   there was chance enough
in each our prise   that we could
involve ourselves   we do know
indeterminate   where to go

38

As follows   what of feeling
fallow drained   to sea with kelp as
fellow to a sleep   no sleeping
why in human terms   and why if
these are all we have   not let
the rest be as it is   sea
its seaness   rock to be understood
nothing   other   rock   in rock terms
no mastery   we might stand
just aside   abashed at fellow
look   an orison   speak only of the self

39

Not miracles   not magic   not
a logic   through no miracle
we survived so long   one pre-
mise   surmised   that we
would know enough   enough to tend a lighthouse
keep off the shoals   pure magic
shoals and how we avoided some
how others foundered   ships we
no longer remember   jewels of the sea

corroded or petrified   into other jewels
shark's eye seeing   and a logic
prisoner of its own short sight
might long for an open boat
unsteady currents

                    40

Damage accrued
                    figured in terms
damage and accrual
                    what is
this world
            alien
without an ability
                    all such words
ours
        sown and reaped

We have nothing
                    but the words
a world
            not known yet
to walk there
                    leave no print
    or leave it
                    lessened

                    41

How do I use the term   I
ask a question   it is not rhetoric
I have tried   find nothing here
or what I found   sounding that word/said
pro found   drops a pebble
into a dark well   falls
finally   how do I   I did not step
no I could not find   a term

                    327

or how a pebble   keep several
handy   saves a day   a life
dropped   slowly   into its own pulse
real thing   how do their terms arrive

42

Cave to crystal   it is midnight in the rock
the mid of myriad faults   crevice
ledge   not equal to its task   it
touches abbreviation   and lengthening
we know   and we do not know
false to predict   yet sanity
precludes avoiding it   rock or water
leaving each other   baring fault   what
we call the fault   yet do not know
way in or out   we break delicate poise
it is made unequal   persists in naming balance

43

To see   in the way a poem sees
that would be better than usual seeing
not an easy way   to see   some
would call it clouded   never having focused
to see what is difficult   necessary
to survive   a poem which will not reason
or project   it tries only for what it says
in what is   yet the failure
of the poem   too   but that is not
the whole of it   the poem may fail
as anything   there is the chance
burst out of   I do not know this place
I am merely here   the poem here

44

Of wreckage   the light where it ends
splintered ends   what is not
is   they are the same thing
caught in a shell of air   a light
nacreous clothing   cloud above
wreckage   this ship foundered
I do not know when   circumstances
interest me   but unnecessary
detail inherent   in this wavering solid
wavering light   under their own circumstances
wreckage alone and not alone
wrecked air and light   of storm tossed
foremost

45

Not adequate to include   or destroy
for simplicity   for direction   erect
barriers   they are impermanent   only
sketched   allow a sail   to catch
before falling   it is a way in
or out   if the outside is remembered
it is not dark   not light   not
anything we propose   determined
not to determined   it is only
what it is   we are   and are not
its congeners

46

What of this fate
                    is nearly
an end which
                    cannot end
a beginning
                    the weird

of fate
        or norn knowing
what is always
                the exacting
words we made
                will not
help us more
                than help
is hope
        to be   or
stay in trace
                which we do not
we cannot help
                or fly
this simple place
                of quits
of fate we'd do well
                        acknowledge
or take another way
                as fate's
acknowledgement

47

Appeal   as loud   as bell clangor
we alone may hear it   it does
not reach the land   or sea
the outriggings   which carry
freight   along a happening   wind
that wind nothing in the sense
of what is beyond it   may
reverse   turn into itself   touch
that small bell   once more
but then we will not   hear
what has been struck   how
reverberant   lost to words
receptors   alone   for signals
where is enough coherence
to sound   a hearing   we have not

48

The intention   not its bravery   there
may be other ways   invention
leads intent   despair may follow it
we think we know   rest on assumption
wink out   our riding lights in storm
not clear   only to ourselves   knowing them
what we wish to know   it is early
our fortunes late   played out
when there is time   we have determined it
that we will be on time   a landfall
it is reckoning   dead reckoning
there are parts unknown   not destined
frail capsule of the flesh   intended

49

If there is sound   there is other
than that sound   will not answer
yet serve as answer   what I say
allow the word its drift
its splinter   shard of light   nor break
continuous   in flaw   its flowing
as dialect the thought is local
cadence is a movement in itself
this cadence of disclosure
its sound is one   discovered it
is various   donor to receptor
not easily perceived   nor any   thing worth seeing
as a movement from itself the sound
unlaid   unquiet   is discovery

December 23, 1989–January 29, 1990

THE HOUSE OF THE GOLDEN WINDOWS

§ ABENDMUSIK

I

Eyes in memory
                    turquoise and amber evoke
still sound shot
                    give over
quiet house she said
mine is not
                    poor woman
delivering what she had
                    to this quiet house
an outside quiet
                    taken as turn
in remove
                    exultant unto gaiety
                                        quiet
black tree jewel
                    dumb cold
wake froth glistering
                    still sound shot
give over
          an outside quiet
                    delivering what she had
poor woman
          to this house
                    wake froth glistering
mine is not
          turquoise and amber evoke
eyes in memory
                    taken as turn
in remove
          give over
exultant unto gaiety
                    quiet

dumb cold
black tree jewel
                    mine is not
in remove
            quiet
mine is not
in remove
is not mine

evoke and amber evoke
home to this quiet
                    shot sound
still give over
                delivering
what she had
                poor woman
glistering wake froth
                        black tree
jewel
        turquoise amber
remove is quiet
                quiet house
                            she said
outside
        is not mine
turn   remove   quiet

eyes
        evoke
                meaning
quiet give over
delivering what she had
                        in memory
evoke
        quiet
                exultant unto gaiety
mine is not
            she said
quiet
        glistering   wake   froth

jewel black tree
taken as turn
                an outside quiet
dumb cold
           she had
turquoise and amber
                 in remove
mine is not
          quiet house
still sound
        shot
              exultant unto gaiety
in memory
           poor woman
what she had

2

To some height
              climbing from
down from
up
the air around
           appearing cloud
length of day
         for movement
night concealed
reminiscence
still
    creak and latch
fit to imply
          safe journey
mountain's distance
              appearing air
the cloud around
             length for movement
day appearing
         night concealed
still
    safe journey

                    distance
up from
down
reminiscence
                    creak and latch
imply
        some height
                    climbing
appearing length for climbing
concealed still creak
latch fit
            safe journey
distance
                mountain's appearing air
to imply the length of day
still
distance
cloud concealed
                    appearing
some height
                around climbing
up
    to imply distances
creak fit
            length latch
                        safe
distance concealed
                    appearing cloud
distance
still
mountain
                reminiscence
                            journey
length around
                    down
from air
                around mountain
distance
            journey
still

for movement
             to some height
    climbing from
          down to up

3

Eisenach to Lübeck
          Bach to Buxtehude
space of benevolence
        that walk
              as history
not necessary
       should be/should not be
the anecdote
       or music
           this at evensong
level walking
      that both were there
             respect among
                colleagues
Buxtehude to Bach
        the anecdote
space of benevolence
the daughter in marriage
          politely refused
Lübeck to Eisenach
       walk
         benevolence a history
should be
      the anecdote
       respect among colleagues
both were there
at evensong
refused politely
the daughter in marriage
       to Eisenach
         that walk
as history

colleagues in respect
                    the anecdote
should be/should not be
this at evensong
level walking
                    or music
the music of both men
elder as arbiter
                    struck dumb
as history
                    the anecdote
stayed three months beyond his leave
as recorded
                    colleagues in respect
at evensong
                    married the "stranger maiden"
an own cousin
                    elder as arbiter
stands dumb
colleagues in respect
                    the anecdote
                              walking
as history
                    should not be
three months beyond his leave
married the "stranger maiden"
as recorded
as history
                    not necessary
                              should not be
                                        history
space of benevolence
                    that anecdote
Eisenach to Lübeck
                    to Eisenach
level walking
should be respect among colleagues
refused
                    the daughter in marriage
married the "stranger maiden"

an own cousin
struck dumb
colleagues in respect
both were there
at evensong

4

Before dark
make landfall
              that the sightings
take account of reef
                    current sweeping past
estuary
        abrupt turn into the land
light
      set to guide those
of land and sea
            that home is reached
in shadow
paid chain
anchored
        before dark
that warmth come over
              sleep following
paid chain
anchored
make landfall
          before dark
take account of reef
estuary
abrupt turn into the land
set to guide those
of land and sea
light
      that home is reached
sleep following
the warmth
make landfall

paid chain
anchored
        in shadow
lieu
    of land and sea
the lee
      out of wind
current sweeping past
             estuary
take account of reef
abrupt turn into land
light set
      that home is reached
paid chain
anchored
      out of wind
before dark
that warmth come over
the lee
      out of wind
to guide those
of land and sea
in shadow
reached before dark
following
make landfall
estuary
     reef abrupt
turn into land
paid chain
      in lieu
of land and sea
following out the wind
sweeping past
        turn into the land
abrupt reef
light
that home is reached
          set
to guide those of land and sea

before dark
the warmth following
sleep
landfall
paid chain
sightings
take account of reef
sleep
before dark

5

Curve implied
        taken from chorus
                at inception
as delight
want as being
dear talk costs dear
        or bursts
             a song a
curve and touch
        the nerve in blood
ah lair
      the lay
        the test of love
salt bite
and fluid blood
high
no more are lost
let loose
      let dust
        as curve
the rounds away
then night is laid
        curve chorus
at inception lair
ah
the lay
from chorus

                    opposite
        to mingle
                    lay
        high blood
                    the test
        of love
                salt fluid
        bite
        caught up and turned
                                ah

                                    men
        destroyers not the
                                men who moved away
        as love loosed them
                                lost
        bite
                inception's chorus
        burst
        dear talk costs dear
        the night inlaid
        curve rounds away
        no more are lost
                                let dust
        the test of love
                                burst
        love loosed
        a song a
        curve and touch
        implied
                    ah
        want as being
                        ah
        the lay
        the test of love
        dear talk costs dear
        the nerve as lair
        ah chorus
        want
                as being
        curve

                    the rounds away
         in delight
                         ah
         mingle
         ah
                  men
         the night inlaid

Inception: June 1987
February 2–6, 1988

§ MORE THAN SMOKE THIS WATER

plumed evidence
substantial
              drop
level
as Herne's Oak   lately discovered in alien country
hart's head in tree   bound to oak   leathern leaf
winter place
                 evidence water
                                elsewhere
                                         shafted
dross   flotsam upward against   branch
shoreward
             ice flake
                     fretted twig plume
drift against oak
              Herne's
                      leaf bound
                                waters shift
drop evidence
           in
              level alien country
                                past oak hart's
shoreward
           plume twig

                    ice flake
alien
        lately discovered
                    substantial
                            drop
level   as Herne's Oak   lately discovered
leathern leaf   elsewhere   shafted   dross
winter place   shift
flotsam
against branch
in tree bound
waters shift
leaf bound   drift past Herne's Oak   as lately discovered
leathern elsewhere   dross shafted   upward against branch
fretted plume
                ice flake shoreward
evidence water
                waters shift
bound in alien country
                    plumed lately
                            discovered alien
flotsam in tree
as hart's head
shift drift
level
        leaf bound

                        .   .   .

        as
            ice flake
                Herne's Oak
                        shoreward
                                leaf bound
flotsam against branch   elsewhere waters shift
upward
            drift past oak
                    drop
                        substantial
                                evidence

343

alien in tree   leathern leaf
twig plume   dross
hart's head   winter shafted
fretted oak
lately shoreward

. . .

              past
              past leaf
              past
              past water
              past
              past shift
              past oak
              past leathern leaf

. . .

Herne's Oak   lately discovered bound to winter plume
evidence water elsewhere winter place
level evidence in alien country   hart's head in tree
against branch leathern leaf twig plume fretted
shafted
            ice flake
                        elsewhere drift
                                    shoreward
substantial country
lately alien
shafted leaf
as Herne's Oak
                lately discovered
                            in alien country

· · ·

elsewhere
             water
dross
             elsewhere
elsewhere
             flotsam
drop against branch
elsewhere
ice flake
plume
             shafted
plumed
             leaf
                   leathern
                         bound to winter twig
against branch
                   upward flotsam
                                   ice flake
shoreward flotsam   dross   shafted   as water plume
alien drift past substantial place   oak branch
shoreward shift

· · ·

leaf bound branch water country twig place
place fretted place alien leaf

· · ·

             against
             evidence
             against
             hart's head
             against
             tree
             against

winter
against
country
against
alien
against

. . .

bound to drift past water winter oak
twig branch plumed   shift leaf evidence elsewhere
ice flake alien shoreward hart's head drop level
lately
        against
                fretted
                        plume
substantial water
lately alien
shafted twig
as leathern winter

. . .

        discovered
                        in oak
        discovered
                        hart's head bound
        discovered
                        alien tree
        discovered
                        discovered
        water
                discovered
        elsewhere

. . .

ice
    drop
ice
    level
ice
    shoreward
upward
      ice
drift ice
past water evidence
ice place
flake drift
past oak
      ice

. . .

oak past place drift shoreward branch   shafted twig place
country discovered in alien water leathern leaf bound
evidence as Herne's Oak water substantial elsewhere place

. . .

plume
    water place
plumed branch
        place
plume oak
branch twig leaf
plume
hart's head
      tree plume
Herne's Oak
     place
alien country
     place
bound elsewhere

347

water plume
place plume in tree

.   .   .

smoke

Inception: December 19, 1988
January 12–18, 1989
Bowling Green, Ohio

§ SMALL PASTORAL DISPLACED

I INTROIT

Our gold
          not common
gold as light
               in noble frame
the window gold
                  it catches
from the east
                  the window's light
is in the west
             at morning
from the west
                the evening light
is east.
             We see it
as an eye's catch
not to possess
               we cannot
further than the rainbow
foot that holds the span
an arch
           our gold

is common
           to the elements
not common gold
               as rain
in fire
       in earth
in air and water
Symbol   Sulfur
and elixir   .

        2 IDYLL

Iris
        moon eye
netted
breathless pace
quiet pour
deflected light
sound
           far off compass
only stir

        3 INTERMEZZO

So rarely rain
               these years
                           with the sound's
percussive fall
               the seethe
a water stopped
               along the eaves
a quiet house
               try evening the measure
                                       that
the house is glad
it might be
               as the presence

in the house
               is of its measure
gladness.
          So rarely
these years
the light's reflection
                  gild of panes
the morning and the evening
                       were
the same
          of the same day
clearing of storm
clouds' interference
                lessens
                     washed a gold
not common
             goodwill
                upsprung
the deed
the word
           impressive
so rare
          fire to seethe
the room's   uncommon gold

4 SCHERZ

Set the branch
say out no way
no saying
            turn about
drip water
           over fall
an   even swaying
let it be   a dancer
legs at scissor
              bend
how the branch
                 might fall

come uppance

        clear to be

the shadow

       still no way.

5

Just as the oars lie hushed above the water
so the water quitted below the lapstrake hull
where shadow flattens   wave along the drift
not always memory   the surge is on
slips   oil   the trace a little closer
wake that stirs   a hand in tending
balanced that the oars are ready
should a wind arise and break this dream
the landfall shore is raised a bit
to ride the sea and all outriders rigged
the news   a bird's cry following
on doom of bell   the steadied buoy
above the shoal   and sun to rise again
the gilded windows   island homestead
stead the house   to follow there the drifting.

6 RECITATIVE

Suffer an elixir that the gild is common   oh uncommon
gold   the window is the best as seen at distance   house of
the golden windows   wind's eye open to a sweep of air that
dries what is not past the water   eye will lighten it

7 AIR

Like a bell

       a bell

its own likeness

        tuned

the metal
   felt the stop
the wave
   long stopping
ürsprach
   upsprung
the gold in
   lightness
how a bell
   is like
it fastens
   on the dome of air
down
   and farther
down

8 LEADING TONES

 elixir
   common
 is uncommon
 gild
 the window
 at a distance
 pane of east
 or of west
 sea mew
 calling
 over island
 once said
 unspoken
 raise to horizon
 time ripened
 the bell
 at angle
 follows wake
 in furrow
 a loneliness
 that sound

of doing
light essence
gold or sulfur

9 RESOLUTION

Let it not
          impersonal
flare   of lightness
                    not common
gold   as light
              the noble frame
of window
              gold
                    caught east and west
morning and evening
                    of the day
the same
          percussive
wavelength
          lap of bell
washed   a gold
not common
                    rainbow arch
an arch as rain in fire
earth in water
symbol elixir
gold and sulfur
eye caught
          iris moon
silence
          hull and drift
steadied buoy to shore
hush of water drip
Let it not
          impersonal
let it
          not impersonal
light from window

                              unto window
    gild a day
                another
    as another day.

                                    Inception: January 14, 1989
                                    January 25–30, 1989

TRIPTYCH 1990

§ ABERRANT ROCK

I

Erratic   dour stone   willing
howe   down it opens
                        deftly
incandescent   stasis   black dike
flowing   cools last wears first
a seemly block   seamed other
dense in tissue   foremost sand milled
faulted
            down
                    willing
                            stone
opens howe
flowing stasis
seemly
other faulted
tissue
dense milled
                    foremost
last first
            wears cools

354

deftly
        deftly incandescent
        block
            and
            seemly dense
other howe opens foremost
willed fault
        presumed
erratic

2

            dour
            block
            seemly

stone dense

        stasis

tissue faulted
sand incandescent
dike   block
howe   down
          opens

3

opening at the howe
hinged stone

care to raise
disturb no map
the ancestors

            bone hint
            no bone

cell by cell replaced
jewel in its own waters
crystal dispersing
                      burials
           stone   at hinge   bone
           no bone cell   jewel
           crystal burial
                            dispersing care
           hinged raise
disturb   no cell   no bone   no stone   no jewel   no waters
crystal   no map   no ancestor
                            care
                            raise
erratic
          stone
              deftly
flowing incandescent
                                    block
                                  seamed
                                  sand
                                  foremost
              milled jewel   dense in tissue
              foremost
                    faulted
              stone hinge bone cell jewel
              crystal
              disturb
              raise
              howe   block
              erratic   map
              milled   foremost
              sand faulted
first
last   cools/ wears   equivalent

4

stone
stone willing
        erratic
            flowing

black dike
milled tissue
dense blocks
howe opening
        fault
           foremost

seamed opened
incandescent
        hinged
          care

map   bone
jewel stone
fossil cell
      dispersing
         waters

ancestors disturb fossil
no cell its own
burials willing
bone block
       erratic
         stasis
hint   replaced
cell   crystal
     stasis

5

caught pocket   loose water
           over stone

long shadow   longer ice
                        sealed prisoner
old wounds   the oldest   woods ignored
                                        found holding
dwarf spell   sweet berry
                        dew distilled and cloud
rain's socket

            loose shadow   over stone
            long wounds   woods ignored
            sweet berry   pocket dew
            the oldest prisoner   dwarf holding
            ice socket   spell
            caught   rain's wounds
            water pocket   found clouds
                                    old oldest
                                    berry spell
                                    sweet distilled
longer long loose

            stone
                    holding
            ice dwarf
                        prisoner found
            woods shadow
                            over spell
            caught sweet berry
                                dew
            holding spell prisoner
            old wood   erratic dour
            stone howe opens
                                incandescent
            seemly block
                            dense tissue
            faulted
                        opening hinged stone
            berry sweet   dew and cloud
            dwarf spell
                        first last

deftly willed
black dike
sealed prisoner
longer shadow
hint   bone cell
crystal
disturb no howe
disturb no ancestor
incandescent care
cools long longer
                    last and first
disturb to raise
              ancestors map
                         bone hint
jewel crystal   seemly incandescent spell
dispersing   distilled sweet berry   socket
water   caught pocket
                      stasis
       burials

                6

Storm touch   cloud higher spaces
black fog   changing maps
ancestral bones laid bare
as crystal darkens   sweetness lost
this spell on open rock   passes

sun silvers   fissure rivulets
brightness
                    erratic blaze
bare
       touch
bones
         storm
spell
       fog
black
       darkens

rock
      passes
crystal
        lost
              sun silvers

cloud silvers rivulets
lost spell this sweetness
fog   black silver
                    ancestral maps
bones
          changing passes brightness
fissure spaces cloud
this stone erratic silvers sun
higher spaces opens rivulets
touch fog maps   changing rock
spell passes   blaze slivers
erratic fissure spaces crystal
brightness darkens bare ancestral bones

pocket caught higher
                  raise care
disturb no shadow
              ice prisoner
jewel dispersing light
                in oldest woods
rain dwarf sweet being's spell

    socket
        distilled
            dew
   cloud
        changing
            maps
   bone blaze
   replaced fossil
         cell by cell
             sweet berry
   ice wounds ignored
         oldest cloud

                no howe hinged
                                dense fog
                                                tissue
                fissure passes
                                dispersing rivulets
                                                        sun erratic
                silvers brightens
                                caught burials
                aberrant erratic
                                stasis
        willing stone
        howe opening
        loose pocket
        higher cloud

                        space blaze
                        woods dew
                        map replaced
                        block faulted

        dour woods
        fog spell
        ignored crystal
        milled sand
        disturb jewel
        sealed stasis
        ancestral blaze
        tissue foremost
        woods ignored
        map bones

                        own waters
                        spell fog
                        burials dispersing
                        berry clouds
                        open touch
                        rock passes sun
                        silvers block
                        sealing storm
                        faulted water

black dike seamed
cools last
wears first
milled

Storm touch   stone willing
incandescent howe   fossil bone replaced
waters jewel   ignored spell sweet
distilled dispersed   replaced
rain's ice socket   rock passes
cloud space opens   sand block milled dense
raise map ancestral hinge   stone care
sun silvers rivulets   erratic tissue blaze

cools

Inception: October 19, 1989
April 30–May 4, 1990

§ WORD / LOGOS

In these beginnings   archaic   lost in light
dust   bitumen spices   breathing
lest the color fade   preserving air   ajar as oils
song speech   prepare   the sound
in foundering the way   was left
archaic breathing air   light beginnings
the dust in foundering way   lest color fade   preserving sound
ajar as sound   lost song speech   prepare beginnings
dust in sound   prepare the way   beginnings lift
oils spices   preserving color   lest breathing fade

give word in these beginnings!

Archaic light   bitumen dust   left breathing song
lost foundering   color spices   sound ajar

fade speech   ajar as oils   these breathings
lost air in color   sound the song   speech was left
light the word   as spices dust   ajar the color
lest dust prepare   the air as sound   foundering breath
the lost in breathing   fade lost song   beginning
fade in air   this sound prepare   the song
in light beginnings   archaic breathing   dust for air

                    word in these beginnings   give!

Dark in flux
the word abroad   on waters
voice in wind   concerted heat abroad
left there in being
                    rise

                         rise up
who here the entrance will   burst voicings
joy before the land
the voice was not
                    in wind
in waters flux
                    give in these beginnings   word!

Abroad the waters
                         heat
                                   a voice
rise here
              to entrance   well in being
rise   voices burst   before the land
in joy   dark void   let these rise up
was not in void   in entrance
                                   will
before the land   concerted heat

                    as breath   as voicing   conquer light!

Joy before the land   burst voices   rise up
in entrance waters   heat in entrance   will rise
before the end   the voice concerted   let rise
up before entrance   in being left   in joy rise here

enjoined as joy   before the voices   wind in flux
dark abroad in being   burst voicings   word was not
on land   on waters   on entrance
voicings   joy   rise up in being
end before end   end burst   end entrance
voices heat   voices flux   wind voices

       conquer light as breath

dark in flux   the word abroad
on waters
one voice in wind
concerted heat abroad   in voices
water/wind   in being   let these rise
who here to entrance will   was not   the void
before the land   the voicings   light
in breathing rise   rise up
the joy before the land   voice in will
will   dark in flux

       conquer breath   conquer light!

Archaic   lost light   breathing
bitumen spices   dust   lest color fade
song prepare   speech   light
beginnings   in foundering   song was light
burst voicings   before the land   the void
wind joy   song joy   heat joy
joy concerted   joy in being   joy rise up
voicings   voice was not   speech
light sound   light ajar   light color
who here to entrance will prepare the sound
       word conquer these beginnings

lost sound   prepare the word   prepare
beginnings   water   light
land   voicings   air
breath song   speech
oils   color   dust

air   sound fade   sound rise
prepare song   prepare spices   prepare joy
burst heat   concerted burst   abroad
who here to entrance will prepare the sound
give flux in wind   give being   voice abroad
foundering was left   dark in way   lest color
fade the air   rise up   abroad in wind

                    ἐν ἀρχή

Or hear voice being   voice before the land
on waters   voicings   concerted void
heat flux   bitumen   spices
wind   song   founder
joy before the void   before the song preserving
speech was left   archaic   lost
light song   speech breathing   concerted song
burst joy to entrance   hear foundering
land   air   waters
void   was not

                    ἐν ἀρχή

In these beginnings   dust
In these beginnings   flux
in these beginnings   light
in these beginnings   color
in these beginnings   land
in these beginnings   waters
in these beginnings   air
in these beginnings   lost lest sound
in these voicings   burst
lost lest voicings   these beginnings
lost lest voicings   breathing
lost lest voicings   joy

                in these beginnings

Who here the entrance will

prepare the void!
give word in these beginnings
breath   conquer light
prepare the void
give joy before the land!

ἐν ἀρχή ἦν ὁ λόγοδ

Inception: July, 1990
December 9–30, 1990

§ LA FOLIA

In triples   threads
bridge three

         openings among

triple once
make mention
move away

         forma antiqua
         (Iberian)
         set spacing
twice as three
break

         set threads
         bridge once
         triple make mention
once
thrice

         thrice
         break
mention move away openings among
triples
threads
bridge

                              move there
                              among
                              break
thrice
                              set spacing

Bridge
              set spacing
                              (Iberian)
forma antiqua
twice as three
once/thrice

bridge threads
among openings
make mention
                        move away
                        bridge triple
                        threads this break
move three
break
(Iberian set)
                        spacing
                        thrice bridge
                        openings

once

In triples threads bridge three openings
among triples over
make mention
                        move away
                        once/thrice
                        forma antiqua
(Iberian) set spacing twice as three break
through diaphanous
imagined breath
                        impulse
                        reckoned
                        voluntary

involuntary
relapse
another
                    other sense
                    lapse
                    triune
voluntary impulse reckoned involuntary
another
lapse other bridge

hence
darkened
spirit
                    diapason
                    diaphanous
                    implies
                    (Iberian)
                    bridge
{ once
{ thrice
                    diaphanous
                    diapason
                    thoroughfare
(three)
in triples opening among diaphanous breath
relapse another other sense a time in triples
threads

thoroughfare
three
openings
                                        diapason
                                        deus vult
implies
hence
darkened
                                        spirit bridge
forma antiqua
                    triples as
                                        diaphanous

368

{ once
{ thrice
                                  move twice
                                  as three

  particle
  diaphanous
  breath
                 hence darkened spirit!
                                breath twice
                                set spacing
      through imagined impulse break triune
  openings
  among triples
  diaphanous threads
                                triples bridge
                                move away
                                make mention

  Threads bridge
  three
  openings

                                among
                                thrice
                                forma antiqua

  diaphanous spirit
  relapse
  at impulse

                  Voluntary   involuntary stasis set spring lapse
  (Iberian)
  time
  stress
  triples
  threads
                                once opening
                                threads another
                                move away
                                openings
                                make bridge
                                mention thrice
                                break breath

{ once
  thrice

                             deliberate
                             mistake
                             thrice mentioned
triples among openings make mention
move away once thrice
(Iberian)   forma antiqua
set spacing   twice as three
breaks through diaphanous
imagined breath
                       no
lapse   hence darkened
involuntary triune
move away   other sense
bridge   openings   spirit
threads triples

three
threads
bridge

                             move forma antiqua
                             thrice another
                             other sense
spirit among set spacing breath
triples
            opening

Inception: 1981
September 20–November 27, 1990

§ STILL HOUR

Long day alone   for one
                              one's all
the loneness   playing
oracle of season's
                         evening of the first
little
snow
                    a timing
bone   hard pressed   one's all alone
gehen sie   gehen
                         ganz allein?

Long day   stillness   one alone
of season's oracles   first a timing
evening   the little bone
                              hard pressed
is all alone   snow   gehen sie
snow   the first a timing
                         gehen   ganz allein?

Alone for one   once playing
loneness little first
                         of snow
the oracle
               a timing
lone day   for one   all playing season
ganz allein?

For one   the playing day
alone   one's all
snow timing   loneness
hard pressed   evening oracle
season's first   one's
all alone

und gehen
                    gehen sie
allein?

Shadow's firming   frozen spray
alone   first season's oracle
a freeze of color   /out/   in pressure
all is loneness   playing   little snow
always for one   as evening of the first
an oracle   a shadow's pressure
firming   darkness overspread   a magic
once the playing oracle
gehen sie ganz allein?

Dew's cast   as early morning
firming shadow's frozen spray
alone for one   the oracle   first of season's
color   out   all loneness playing
shadow's alone   alone alone
gehen shadow   season sie   oracle ganz
allein
                    for one alone
                              hard pressed bone
a shadow's   firming
alone   the loneness playing   timing
snow   or little evening
one's   all alone   freeze of color
out alone   bone's pressure   long
lone day   of color pressure   freeze
evening   playing pressure   timing
dew's shadow   all pressure   oracle
gehen sie   ganz   allein?

Long day alone   for one   one's all
the loneness   oracle of evening   season's playing
loneness   for one   first little snow
hard pressed   freeze of color   in pressure
out   a timing
gehen sie   (one's all)   ganz allein?
                    (for one)

firming
shadow
alone
evening
snow
color
freeze
bone
oracle
gehen?

long
for one
day
all
alone

little
season's
playing
pressed
sie?

bone
frozen
hard
first
loneness
out
pressure
spray
frozen
ganz allein?

Long day alone   for one
                              one's all
the loneness   playing
oracle of season's
                    evening of the first
little
snow

                          a timing
bone   hard pressed   one's all alone

Dew's shadow   all pressure   oracle
gehen sie   ganz   allein?

Firming   a shadow   one's all
alone   bone freeze   color
out   at   timing
of season's oracle   first a loneness
alone for one's   once playing   first
a snow   hard pressed
                                (tone)   color
long alone
                    all loneness
                                        playing
little
snow
            a timing
gehen   gehen   ganz allein?

This freeze of color   this pressure   out
this long day   alone for no one   this little snow
this evening   one's all   playing alone

This shadow's firming   this frozen spray
this dew's timing   this hard pressed bone
this evening colored   this in loneness
That alone   that little evening   that playing
that once and first   that long shadow   that season's
of color   of bone   one's loneness

Freeze this color
                        that
of this long day alone
                            for one
that one's all
            in loneness
be
        (this)

374

oracle of season's
                evening
of the first little snow
one's all alone
                this color
out bone pressure
gehen   gehen   ganz
        allein?

Alone for one   day long   all loneness
playing oracle   a timing snow   hard pressed
out firming   spray   in shadow's freeze
bone the loneness   one's alone   all color
gehen sie   ah gehen   ganz allein?

Inception: April 1991
May 18–August 1, 1991

§ ATONEMENT

Return
a guest   wind around returning
sense or side
sentient   largesse a debt
made over
forgive us then   transgression
here to give
spell once a spelling   hold the guest
return a story
wind returning sense   side and wind
sentient
debt   largesse   to give
here spell once a spelling
return transgression
forgive   us

hold

guest
here to give
made over
wind
returning   debt

sentient   wind   guest
forgive us   debt   give
                      a story

hold wind around
transgression
spell
        side sentient
re   turning

sentient   the guest
debt forgive us   hold transgression
story spell   once   a spelling
            (more)
wind senses   side
            largesse
return the guest here
        (oh)

forgive us

hold in spell
largesse
made over
spelling debt
to give a story
hold
hold once
hold sentient the wind
around us hold
hold silent guest
to give transgression
hold   forgive   us

Bind held close
        a talisman

                              in burning wreath
a ravening
              a choking salt
                              a cleansing
rime of the seas
              death's indenture
                                        now
forgive us now
                    return a story
now

burning wreath   burn talisman   bind transgression
ravening largesse   to give a debt   in ravening
indenture guest   indenture wind around
sentient held close   a burning   choking salt
cleansing wreath   cleansing talisman   cleansing debt
transgression given   a ravening story   hold and return
rime of the sense   silent transgression
forgive us   cleansing   forgive a debt

spell spelling
talisman held close
wreath a ravening
a bind
a burning
spell
transgression
spell debt
spell a story
a wind around
a cleansing
forgive death's impetus

hold as held
close
        bind
a burning rime
sentient guest
ravening transgression
hold silent
choking

forgive us debt
Of sense a story   cleansing
talisman   burning wreath
ravening spell
once hold
largesse a guest
return wind returning
bind sense   forgiveness
choking salt
death's rime of seas
inception now
returns a debt
a burning wreath a ravening
forgive
            forgive us now

cleansing   burning   spelling
inception sentient
here to give transgression
largesse a debt
forgive us guest
forgive us story
here to return   in wind
silent spell

forgive us
            now
forgive us debt   here give transgression
hold

Return   a guest   wind around returning
sense or silent   sentient   largesse a debt
made over   forgive us them   transgression
here to give   spell once a spelling   hold the guest
return a story

Bind held close   talisman
a burning wreath   ravening   a choking salt
cleansing   rime of the seas
death's inception   forgive us now

returns a story
Held binding
a debt
a burning wreath
rime of the seas
salt choking
a wind around sense
a story   hold
here to give
a story
largesse returns
forgive us now
death's ravening
forgive us then
sentient talisman
a silent spell
around
       us

hold burning   hold ravening
hold spell and wreath
rime seas   a debt   a salt
forgive us   bind us
guest come sentient
indenture story's salt
transgression   wind returning
forgive us then
forgive us now.

Inception: August 8, 1991
September 15, 1991–October 12, 1991

§ IT TAKES ME SOME TIME

(Allen Ginsberg to Charles Reznikoff:
   Old sage Reznikoff,
   how are you at rhyme?
C.R. to A.G.
   Very very good,
   but it takes me some time.)

Ashes
         ashes to ashes
might be beginning
                        ash
a scale
         a shade
                  ashes
unresting
         cadence
                  the opening
                              burn
as to ash
         could be fire
                  pale opening
takes
         (or permits)
it
takes me some time
Offering   pale opening
fire could be a scale
ashes   a shade some time beginning
cadence unresting
as to scale a shade   to ashes
permits a fire it takes
permits scale opening
offering

Sun to cold
sun
cold night

end
beginning
a fire
resting
ferments
our burning
closes   shut
does not   cannot
allow
it takes
me
some time
times a sum
to add
to sum
away from sun
light
ash
it
takes me some time

Post ludens   play
not to play
to cold to sun
to night to ash
to beginning
to a fire   to ash
to ferment   cannot
allow
it takes me some time.
Ashes to ashes
a scale   beginning
sun to cold   night
to a fire
          to ashes
beginning ends   it
does not count sum
ferments
it takes me some time
(quietens .)

might change in order
in order to change
an order
arduous assay
weight becomes
                          might become
as move to move
a shading
fire could become
                          almost
a journey
how one could stand
in order that earth
                          or sand
(might)
blow away
unwavering   footstep
it takes me some time

Some time in order
fire
ash   it
might become
unwavering
footstep
time takes
some
ash blown away
it takes
or could become

Ashes might (not) be
cadence as to fire   unresting
could be pale to opening   permits beginning
sun to cold   away from man
it
      takes me some time

does not

cannot allow
sums or ashes
burn as to fire
could be ash
pale shade
a shade in fire
permits me some time

Lest stroke on stroke
                hammer's blow
be sound or sign
                complete in answer
air of angle
            bird's bill
salt meadows fill
                flow away
to break in altering
                sluice of bearing
impossible lest time it takes
implies
how it takes me

stroke on sign
or blow
stoke angle
air of bird's bill
complete sluice
salt meadows
fill flow
lest time implies
impossible
how it takes me
change in order
as   order
arduous assay
almost ash to journey
suns
lest strike   it
takes me some time

In order   beginning ash
to ashes   unresting
pale opening fire   it takes
sun to cold   it
takes cold night
beginning a fire   it takes some ash
away from sun
light
ash   it
might change   stroke on stroke
lest hammer's blow
complete in air
an angle   bird's bill
answer
fill to altering
lest time implies   it
takes me

Not to cold a sun a shade
lest fire begins our burning
lest cold does not allow
a sum   light   ash it
takes me   some time
it takes

(It)

takes some order
takes some change
takes ash   takes fire
takes journey
takes away   sum and sun
takes cold   takes burning
takes lest change   lest shade
takes   lest blow
hammer   on hammer's blow
takes light   ('s)   beginning
lest altering fill to salt
lest bird's bill   takes
time   implies it takes

stroke on stroke
on hammer   lest and last it
takes me
might   time
cold angle
lest it takes away
it takes me   takes our burning
lest it takes me
                    ask me
some time

Journey ask and sun
                        (light)
altering time   sun and fire
                            (light)
complete angle altering time
it takes
lest impossible
takes me

To cold a fire implies
sun sum beginning
complete in air
it takes ash and fire
sum to sun to time
a fire beginning   takes
cold night   end/beginning
a shade unresting
burn
salt meadows burn to ash
impossible   lest there
could be fire
ash
        (not)
ashes to ashes
unresting
                (revealed)
cadence to ash
pale opening might be
beginning

sun to sum
to resting   to cold   away from
light to fire
to sun
ash it   a shade
stroke on stroke
(arduous assay)
as more to more
in order
earth or sound
in order to change

Dimming of the day
an angle
            broken
answer me

takes
        (oh)
                takes
what
        oh takes
unresting
                takes me some time

Ashes to ashes
dust to dust
fire and light
sum to sun opening
darkness to darkening
takes me some time
to the road and the journey
gives us the rhyme.

Inception: October 8, 1991
October 10–November 24, 1991

Interview

INTERVIEW

The following interview with Theodore Enslin, which serves in place of an editor's preface to this volume, was conducted with the author at his kitchen table on 11 August 1997. The idea of such a dialogic afterword owes its genesis to both Enslin's resistance to the usual critical approach to his work, and the editor's interest in dialogic approaches to history (literary and otherwise) as practiced by Kevin Dwyer (*Moroccan Dialogues: Anthropology in Question*), Dennis Tedlock and Bruce Manneheim (*The Dialogic Emergence of Culture*) and William Carlos Williams and Edith Head's *I Wanted to Write a Poem: The Autobiography of the Works of a Poet*. Readers interested in other interviews with Enslin are encouraged to locate those with Charles Stein & George Quasha (in *Truck* 20), Lee Bartlett (in *Talking Poetry: Conversations in the Workshop with Contemporary Poets*) and Ed Foster (in a special Theodore Enslin issue of *Talisman* #12, Spring 1994), among others.

NOWAK: Well, what I thought we could do, what we've talked about doing, is just to walk through the poems that are going to be in the *Selected,* and you could just tell me a little bit about them.

ENSLIN: Okay.

NOWAK: We started off with "Road or River" and you said, when was that one written?

ENSLIN: It was written in 1943.

NOWAK: And the poems in "The Work Proposed" then go from 1943 . . .

ENSLIN: The actual title poem "The Work Proposed," that was either late '56 or early '57. I'm not sure. I put the thing together, when Cid [Corman] asked, and said if you want to, I'd like to do this one, and I said fine.

NOWAK: So why did you choose that to be the first poem in *The Median Flow*?

ENSLIN: Well, because it's the oldest one that I would really like to keep, and at the same time it's the only one of that period that despite its falterings does show something of the structure of what I was to do later on. It's the reason that I kept it.

NOWAK: And then "Tansy for August," when is that from?

ENSLIN: "Tansy for August" is 1947.

NOWAK: And you've got a story behind that one, right?

ENSLIN: Yes, that is the . . . when I first met Mark Hedden, who was in Olson's last class at Black Mountain. Apparently Olson stormed into class one day and said, "There's some bastard up in Massachusetts writing about

Tansy . . . Tansy is *mine!*" (laughs) And Mark remembered that and said "Oh yes, I know about you." (laughs) And so I don't know, I could have been annoyed, or I could have been sort of cowed by that. But I wasn't, and all I said to Cid when I realized that Olson was unhappy about it was, "Tansy is common enough, I think there is enough for both of us." (laughs)

NOWAK: What about "Witch Hazel"?

ENSLIN: "Witch Hazel," yes, that has an interesting story behind it too. Not actually behind it, but after it came out in the book, that's about 1949, and it actually was one of those poems that probably was gurgling around in me for a long, long time. I wrote it in a space of about six minutes, and I know this exactly, I know exactly where I had been standing in the middle of the road by the house in Temple [Maine] where I later lived that is the beginning of the road up the mountain. When the book came out a gentleman by the name of Thomas Bouchard, actually a very good photographer, but who was fond of going around saying things like "Steiglitz, Steichen, and me!" came to me. (laughs) Actually he did do the first documentary on Martha Graham, and he figured that he was sort of an oracle for things artistic. "Oh, the years that it must have taken you, the sweat and the blood to do this." And I said, "Yeah, actually Tom, I can tell you exactly how it was written. It took me exactly six minutes." He was furious. "We'll never talk about art again!" (laughs)

NOWAK: Then we've got "Notes for a Cold Beginning." When was that written?

ENSLIN: That's a little later, that's probably about 1953-4.

NOWAK: And we've got "The Glass Harmonica" from that selection.

ENSLIN: Yeah, "The Glass Harmonica" is much later. The book was published in 1958, so that was about '57. I know that because that was when I was really friendly with Denise Levertov, and I remember discussing it with her. She liked that one.

NOWAK: And then, what was the initial response to that book when it first came out? Did you hear from a lot of people?

ENSLIN: Boy, I heard from all the people that were connected with . . .

NOWAK: *Origin?*

ENSLIN: *Origin,* yes, that was nice.

NOWAK: Who did you get letters from? Do you remember?

ENSLIN: Creeley, Larry Eigner, um . . . Pound.

NOWAK: You got a letter from Pound?

ENSLIN: Uh huh, very nice, very brief. I thought a little off hand, but thinking of things like the government, I think I did pretty well (laughs). And

Marianne Moore. Cid insisted that I send a copy to Marianne Moore and she wrote a very nice letter.

NOWAK: Are those at Buffalo [the Poetry/Rare Books Collection at SUNY], those letters?

ENSLIN: I think the Marianne Moore is. Then it wasn't until later, when Lorine Niedecker's letters were published, that I realized that she was sort of following the stuff and liked it but she never wrote to me, and I've never understood why, and I've understood even less why Cid, who was getting those letters, never told me. I really would have liked to have made that connection.

NOWAK: Then, next thing we're going to use is "New Sharon's Prospect." Can you tell me a little bit about the story behind that?

ENSLIN: Yep. I started that in the fall of '61, when I started visiting the family—the Tibbetts family in New Sharon. And I sent Cid some poems, a number of the poems, a little thing I was doing for myself. He liked them, and he also wrote back and said, "I seem to sense a prose gloss," and actually there was one, though I wasn't thinking of it particularly that way. I kept a journal, and I put in a lot of the stuff that happened at that house, with those people. And so I just picked out pieces that seemed to fit with the poems, and that more or less accounts for the fact that the datings are not consecutive. You get something like October, and then you get September. Yep. And . . . but then after I put together about two-thirds of it, I got a sense of the whole thing, and it was very consciously done, from then, on to the end. In a way I'm a little sorry that it happened quite that quickly. If I hadn't realized until the very end that these two things went together, I might have been able to integrate it a little better. I don't know. I finished it just before I went for my year in New York. Three days before, I remember very well. Up on the mountain I was, it would've been about . . .

NOWAK: Came out in '62.

ENSLIN: It came out in '62, so yeah, that was the fall. It came out in the fall of '62, after I had come back, so it was probably January, and had the business in the last poem, "he shook his head," watching the snow storm coming. I know that was about Christmas time.

NOWAK: When you were writing that, besides Cid's comments, were you feeling like . . . were you thinking at all of Williams, and *Spring and All, The Descent of Winter,* any of that?

ENSLIN: Well of course that stuff has always been very much an influence. I don't know that I was thinking of it. I was thinking, as you joke, (laughs) of *Let Us Now Praise Famous Men* towards the end, and then I really wanted to integrate it and I remember thinking of William Wood and *New England's Prospect*. I didn't have my copy then, I know it was still on the Cape. I finally got it back. I remember going out to the College Library in Farmington to find it, and check out things, make sure that I was doing it accurately.

NOWAK: And you were saying that the people it's about actually read it and you got a response from them.

ENSLIN: (laughs) This was about ten years later, and one of the twenty-eight children called and was not very friendly. I apparently . . . I don't imagine he had read the whole thing, but he had read enough to say, "That book you wrote made the old man out as a *pauper*." (laughs) And I tried to sort of soothe ruffled feathers, and I said, "You know, I really tried to be very kind to him. I was very much impressed with your family because it's unique." But he didn't like it, and he said, "I'm going to send my mother. I'm going to send her to that bookstore in Farmington and she'll get every copy and burn it!" Well of course that bookstore didn't carry it. (laughs) And I never heard anything more about it. On the other hand, as you know, I've gotten a little sick hearing about it and for some reason, it caught on in a more general way then anything else that I ever wrote, and I don't know why.

NOWAK: I even heard Silliman praising it recently [on the Poetics LISTSERV out of Buffalo].

ENSLIN: Exactly. (laughs) Praising in a way that indicated very clearly that he never read anything else. (laughs) But anyway, what it is, it stands there and . . . .

NOWAK: You really haven't done much else like it.

ENSLIN: It's something I'm very glad that I did. I would not want to do anything else like it.

NOWAK: Next thing . . . We took some pieces from *The Place Where I Am Standing*, which was . . . Jim Weil did it, right, and was that the first book he did by you?

ENSLIN: Yes.

NOWAK: Took a couple pieces, and that book comes from '64, and we took the "Pavane for William Carlos Williams." Got anything to tell me about that?

ENSLIN: Nothing, except that I knew that Williams was just about at the end, and I can't remember very much else.

NOWAK: Did you ever hear from him, from the earlier pieces? Did you have any correspondence with Williams?

ENSLIN: No. I never had any correspondence, but I talked with him quite a lot. It was after *The Work Proposed* came out, when I was living in New York, on Fifteenth Street. Denise Levertov, Mitch Goodman, they urged me to call Williams and go out there. He knew who I was, yes.

NOWAK: And you go out to Nine Ridge?

ENSLIN: And I went out to Nine Ridge, and apparently hit it off because he invited me back for a number of weekends. It was Friday afternoon. Floss baked cookies.

NOWAK: And how were the cookies?

ENSLIN: The cookies were good! (laughs)

NOWAK: Then we've got "Song in the Mood." Anything behind that poem that you can remember? [clock, an old regulator, chimes twelve times in the background] And then we also took "An Afternoon Like This" and "I Say There'll Be Music." What was the reaction to that book when it came out?

ENSLIN: That of course came out after I had gone to New York and met a lot of people with whom I had been corresponding for years, and they more or less knew me and were interested. So there was quite a lot of response to it. And the best one, of course, was the letter from Oppen, which...

NOWAK: Was that your first letter from Oppen?

ENSLIN: Yeah. I had met Oppen through Diane Wakoski and David Antin, and we liked each other. And then I started really to read him, at Diane's urging actually. I mean, yeah, I knew the name, but I didn't know... both *The Materials* and *This In Which* had come out at that time. Anyway, I sent him a copy of *The Place Where I am Standing* and the letter is very very short. I've still got it framed somewhere. [Robert] Bertholf isn't going to get that for awhile. (laughs) And all it says is, "Dear Ted, Dear Distant Ted. If the blaze of intention holds up, we share a common country. Acting ceremoniously as the elder. George." I thought, "Well, maybe it was worth it!" (laughs)

NOWAK: So you've got that framed somewhere?

ENSLIN: Yep, but I don't know where. I think... I had it up in Temple, and I know I brought it. But I think it's in what I call a memorabilia box, which is in the attic room, the crawl space that goes back in there, and this box which is about six feet long, wood. It looks like a coffin. My father used to use it to send books from the winter house to the Cape and back again every year. He made it. I got a lot of stuff in there, and I think that's where it is.

NOWAK: Then, let's see... The next book that we're going to use some poems from is *This Do and The Talents,* from 1966. And I think we've talked about it a couple of times and I only had one piece, there in the beginning, and

393

then we talked about putting in a few more, and I came up with "For Susan With Sunflowers," "A Little Night Music," "The Belongings" and "This Do, In Remembrance" . . . tried to pick some pieces that sort of went together.

ENSLIN: Well, of course it all goes together. That in a way has a kinship with "New Sharon," because I wrote them both more or less with the same idea in mind: trying to explain something to myself that I didn't quite understand. In the case of "New Sharon" it was, "Well what the hell is it that keeps this family together?" And in the case of "This Do" it was a very bittersweet relationship with a woman of whom I'm still very fond. But what is it that really prevents it from having a complete relationship? "The Belongings," that poem in particular, takes that up. Talking about all the objects in her room, and her life seems to be there, but not in her. And again and again it comes up in the poems. Everything is here, but there is nothing here.

NOWAK: When we talked about . . . I think . . . the first list that we came up with, with some poems that *had* to be in there. One of them that you mentioned was "To Come To Have Become," which came out in '66, and we put in the whole thing, we're going to put that in complete. Why did you feel it was important that that be in there complete?

ENSLIN: Well, because those were . . . I was very certain of all those poems, and Jim Weil *theoretically* published that. He had very little to do with it. You'll see that it was printed in Japan, and Cid agreed with him to bring it out. You can't move a thing, everything is right. And I still feel it is. It's really almost a farewell, to . . . sort of an early period.

NOWAK: How would you describe the style of that early period?

ENSLIN: Well, obviously, it was very much influenced by Williams. Every once in a while I would get into line structures because of things that I was hearing which certainly were not Williams. But about the time you say that you've got something completely your own, you'll find that about twenty other people have been working independently in exactly the same direction. What Zukofsky used to say again and again, "It's in the air," and I think that is true. I think that people in a particular period, working quite independently, pick up on very common things. That is what makes the hallmark of that period. It's not the particular crotchets of this school or that school, it's things that are really pretty much beyond the control of any serious artist in any field. You write from your own period. You paint from your own period. You compose music. I've often said to people who intone the litany, "I don't like modern art." "Well, you don't like the art of your period." Maybe the reason is that you don't like your period, because the artist at this point is powerless. If he is doing a responsible job, he is using the materials of his own period. He is also using everything that has gone before, and if the particular piece is of great enough stature, it in a very curious way probably foreshadows everything that is to come. I mean these are the great landmarks, but really the individual has very little control over that.

NOWAK: Do you think that *To Come To Have Become* was the first book that you achieved that sort of . . . where everything felt right? Or do you think that you achieved that earlier?

ENSLIN: Well, I think that is probably true of "This Do," but that was simple because of the chronology. But yeah, I would say as a book made up of individual pieces that were not consciously linked at the time of the writing. Yes, I would say that was the first time I really felt, "Good! I've done this."

NOWAK: In the next book, we took a selection from *The Diabelli Variations and Other Poems.* We took "The Log of the Divided Wilderness."

ENSLIN: Okay, now these were very much earlier. Actually, did you use *The Median Flow* version? Yes you did, okay. [Robert] Kelly published the whole of it including "The Diabelli Variations" themselves. He did a little series of books called Matter Books, and that has the whole thing. I decided eventually that I like some things about the Diabellis. Actually that was the first time that I used a musical title, and did in some ways something analogous to the Beethoven series of variations. What Beethoven did was to take what he felt, and what many other people felt, was an extremely inferior jingley tune, a waltz by Diabelli, who had sent this thing out to fifty composers and wanted them to write variations. One or two variations, and then he would . . . he was a publisher, and he would publish the whole thing and everybody would clean up. Well, it more or less did work that way. Beethoven at the time was working on the "Missa Solemnis" and the Ninth Symphony and wasn't much interested, and he certainly thought it was a very inferior piece . . . tune. But eventually, he turned to it and said, "Hmmm. Well, I have the technique, and I have the knowledge. I can make a set of variations on this thing, and I'll show that silly little fool what you can do even with something as inferior as his waltz." And so he wrote this immense thing, the Thirty-three Variations. I certainly (laughs) wouldn't feel contemptuous of my daughter as I would of somebody like Anton Diabelli! But she was about four or five, something like that, and she was skipping rope and she made up a little jingle, "Race me there, race me there" um . . . something . . . "you know where." I can't remember the whole thing. And I kind of liked it, and I said, "Well . . ."

I was just dimly aware then of what became very important to me later. The value and importance of variation in all art. And that was the first time that I tried to do that. And that was published first in the *Quarterly Review of Literature*. I told you that little story. I got paid for it! Then . . . "The Log of the Divided Wilderness" actually is a sort of sequence thing. My whole idea of sequence actually came quite early. I wrote many sequences, most of which have been destroyed, thank god, until the late ones. But I became fascinated with the idea of a sequence, the kind of sequence that I later worked with from reading Rilke . . . like the *Stundenbuch, The Book of Hours.* Or the *Buch Der Bilde.* Those immense things. And then the *Duino Elegies,* or the *Sonnets.* These are all sequential works. The idea being that the individual segments are possible alone, but they make very very much better sense if they are . . . if you take the entire structure. And you see, because even though maybe nothing particularly striking is brought back, there are elements brought back, in each section, and they do work in a complete structure.

NOWAK: Which is equally very musical.

ENSLIN: A very musical idea, and I was becoming more and more aware . . . That of course was either '59 or '60.

NOWAK: "The Log of the Divided Wilderness" came out?

ENSLIN: Yeah. I can't remember when it was. It didn't come out, that's when I wrote it, but I was . . . I was beginning to be quite aware of the fact that the musical training that I had had was something that I was using in the writing of poetry, and that there were many things that I could use there. And that was when I started (laughs) to be a little annoyed with the rather cavalier use of musical terms by many poets. They talk about cadence, but very few of them, of course there are some that do, very few generally know exactly what a cadence is, in musical terms. And if you say something . . . but they really don't know what the principles are. And if you said, "Well, I like that plagal cadence that you used," the guy will look at you, "Huh?" He doesn't know what a plagal cadence is. (laughs) And I began to get ideas. One of the ones that happened just about the same time that I wrote "The Log of the Divided Wilderness," maybe three or four months later, I got the idea of antiphony, and antiphonal sound. I had been listening to a lot of Andrea and Giovanni Gabrieli, and their great students Monteverdi and Heinrich Schütz. They had this idea of antiphonal sound, which they developed simply from the vehicle which they had, which was the nave of St. Marks Cathedral in Venice, which has magnificent reverberating acoustic which is a natural for that kind of sound. As a matter of fact, both poets and musicians have used St. Marks ever since. And it is open now, you can go and talk to people. There's a horn player I know who used to go at midnight, he was given permission to go in and play his horn. Anyway, I wanted to use antiphonal sound, and I started in on something . . .

[TAPE BREAK]

NOWAK: So it didn't work?

ENSLIN: So it didn't work! And it took me twenty-five years until it did work, and then as I told you this morning, I remember that was just before I left the Cape. But I was up on the Mountain and I sweat blood over that thing, and finally I just dumped it. And then, twenty-five years later, I came back to it. I always had it in my mind. I really would like to do something with this, and I wrote the seventy odd sections of that thing in about four days. I mean, it just poured out like nothing. Apparently I had been thinking subliminally about the thing for the whole time. It took that long.

NOWAK: So is there a sense of a movement when you say . . . I mean, would it be correct to describe it at all as a movement from, like you said, that more Williams influenced work, to a little more Poundian, or that Melopoeia idea?

ENSLIN: Yes. The Melopoeia. Yes. It certainly was. At the same time I never really lost the Williams. I still write little poems that . . . actually a section of a sequence that's being published now, called "Skeins."

NOWAK: Is that the one coming out in Japan?

ENSLIN: Yes. And this is the weird thing. It's some guy who's got a lot of money, and he is giving Cid a magazine within a magazine, and he can use things of size. I really didn't want to contribute to it. But finally, I figured, well, if Cid is willing to do something of this size, fine. It's a little longer actually than "Autumnal Rime," and I wasn't sure. But anyway, he liked it, and he sent me commentary. He sent back a very good editorial letter, questioned all my typos and that sort of thing. He made comments on several sections, and one, he said, "You know, this is very reminiscent of Williams," and I'm sure that that goes on. But yes, I began to expand from that and by the beginning of the '70s, I was experimenting with using musical forms of various kinds.

NOWAK: The next book we took a piece from, and if I remember correctly, I think I had just one or two letters with [John]Taggart. I asked him once or twice what he thought was essential and I think one of the pieces he mentioned, if I remember correctly, was from *Agreement, and Back,* and that's "The Four Temperaments."

ENSLIN: Yep. Oh! He liked "The Four Temperaments"?

NOWAK: I think that's one of the ones that he really stressed.

ENSLIN: Well, that's okay! (laughs) My choice from that would've been "The Dance Poem." No, I'm getting ahead of me in poems which came after that. Well, okay . . .

NOWAK: Any story behind that piece? What do you remember about that?

ENSLIN: "The Four Temperaments." Yeah. Actually, it had musical connections, which was not a musical connection because it was a literary, (laughs), a literary connection with a literary idea in a composition, a composition by Hindemith called "The Four Temperaments." I was listening to it and actually working with the score too, at the time. I really liked that piece, and still like the piece, and well it's fixed. Let's return it to literature from which it came. I didn't realize that that was the piece Taggart liked.

NOWAK: Then, from *The Poems,* what I've got down here is "The Fire Poem" and "The Poem of No Shadow."

ENSLIN: Okay. Yeah. That's a very pretentious title. (laughs)

NOWAK: *The Poems*?

ENSLIN: *The Poems.* Exactly.

NOWAK: Is that, I mean . . . that's the first one that you did that with *Papers,* and you did that with a couple of others.

ENSLIN: Of course. There were a lot of them. Yep.

NOWAK: Is that the first one like that?

ENSLIN: Yep.

NOWAK: What's the theory behind that? Or the idea behind that?

ENSLIN: I don't think I had any particular idea. It was simply that I wrote a number of medium-longish pieces.

NOWAK: Sequences?

ENSLIN: And they fit together in a kind of sequence. Okay. The one that I particularly like, which is not in this, but maybe I like it simply because of the idea, is "The Dance Poem." "The Dance Poem" depends upon something that is very important to me, and because of living in the twentieth century I'm being conditioned by a lot of centuries before. It is pretty much impossible for me, or for most people now, to understand the medieval triune rhythm.

NOWAK: I'd say that'd be difficult for most people.

ENSLIN: It would be very difficult. The thing is, your denominator. Instead of being six-eight time . . . say you had eight-six time. The thing was divided into threes, and the idea was that one corresponded to the voluntary system, the things that we do purposely. Three was involuntary things that we really don't control, heart beat, breathing, though we can control it but it goes on whether we do or not, things of that sort. And then the other one. Number two is the thing, it is ineffable. It is a part of the Holy Trinity. It is the Holy Ghost. It is . . . it gets off into some pretty strange places, but there are certain pieces of music that have come down to us that apparently originally were conceived of this way. We have never heard them that way because very simply we don't think that way. Among them, the one that later I used, "La Folia." "La Folia" originally was probably Portugese, Portugese dance, a rather lugubrious dance, and I have never understood why it should be called "La Folia." The Follies or the Fun. The follies of Spain. Doesn't seem to me the . . . (laughs) It's a magnificent tune. The melody that is being used so many times by so many composers, is still being used, is actually not the original melody, but a descant to it. And of course it is in our contemporary sense of meter. But originally, apparently it was, the denominator would've been three, not four, and in "The Dance Poem" this comes back again and again. I'm using triple syllables and then coming back to the one, three, three, three. That's the reason for it. That was the first time that I ever consecutively worked with something like that. And as a matter of fact, I got all of this, not through any history of art or musicological study, but through a study of medicine. And then I looked up things and found references to it. But it is something that is not very often stressed.

NOWAK: Where . . . like at this time, when the poems came out in 1970, were you on the Mountain then? Were you writing these on the Mountain?

ENSLIN: No. I was down at the other house.

NOWAK: Then we took some pieces from *The Country of Our Consciousness.* 1971. Sumac, did they do that book?

ENSLIN: No, *Sand Dollar.* Sumac did *With Light Reflected.*

NOWAK: The "Canso," for example, and "Listening to Mozart."

ENSLIN: Yep. "Listening to Mozart."

NOWAK: What else do we have here? "Dear Diary," which I think you were surprised that we . . .

ENSLIN: (laughs) Well, I kind of like that poem because it's a sort of macaronic account of my days. It was a very rainy day, in . . . I guess it was about the first of April, but it was warmer than it usually is up there. And I went out by a swamp and actually the red wing blackbirds had come back, and I went back to the house and listened to both the Hammmerclavier and Opus III. The two last sonatas of Beethoven, and I had mackerel for dinner. I remember all of that. The last quote, that was when I was doing the homeopathic studies, and the last thing, the quote, the man sitting in the garden. "Do I see one light or two lights?" as will happen in old age. But that actually comes from a biography of Constantine Hering, who was the . . .

NOWAK: But you were eating mackerel! (laughs)

ENSLIN: But, I was eating mackerel. Yes. Well (laughs) Constantine Hering has always impressed me.

NOWAK: With two R's? H-e-r-r-i-n-g?

ENSLIN: No. It's H-e-r-i-n-g.

NOWAK: Ahhh . . . Okay.

ENSLIN: And he was a very early disciple of Hahnemann, who came to the states and eventually ended in Philadelphia, where he founded the Hahnemann Hospital and Library and Medical School, all of which still exist. Very, very interesting man in many directions. He was the man among other things who introduced Lachesis . . .

NOWAK: Snake Venom!

ENSLIN: Snake venom. He was kicked out of Saxony, where he was . . . he had a history that was sort of parallel to the history of my own Great, Great, Great, Great, Great, Great . . . Grandfather who had a court position and got into trouble and came to America and went to Boston. Hering went first to Surinam. Actually, he was sent there by the Elector of Saxony to make a collection of fauna and flora. But he was far more interested in medicine and he was treating the Natives and anybody who would . . . and then he got fired and he was stranded in Surinam. And among other things, he was beginning to be interested in Snake Venoms (laughs), and he . . . the Natives finally . . . apparently they were very suspicious of this guy, brought him the South American bush master, the largest Rattle Snake, and . . . They did catch one and he did milk it.

NOWAK: Which could not have been an easy task.

ENSLIN: It was not an easy task, and he didn't get bitten, but he cut himself with forceps or something that he had holding the jaws open. And he went into all kinds of things. And they thought he was going to die. And his wife is standing there. But he came out of it finally (laughs) . . . poor Constantine, Constantine! He said, "What did I say? What did I say? What did I do?" because he was making a . . . proving of the substance, and he introduced it to . . . That one milking actually lasted the entire profession for eighty years.

NOWAK: Wow!

ENSLIN: And the second milking was done by Raymond Ditmars, who was the big reptile guy in New York. I have an account of that somewhere. But all that collection was supposed to go to the Elector of Saxony. He had somehow or other . . . Hering got to Philadelphia and he made a present of that to the Academy of National Science. And when I was doing this I was very thorough, and I called them up and said, "I would like to see the Hering collection." (laughs) And they thought, "Well, we do have some fish." And I said "No, no, no, no, no." "Oh yeah! Well I think we got that down in the cellar somewhere." And they did. And I went and I saw the actual snake. He was taken out of his bottle from the formaldehyde, and the guy said, "I don't think that this thing's been changed in about eighty years." (laughs) And then he put some fresh formaldehyde in and put it back. (laughs). So that's a long explication, but anyway, that's who that is.

NOWAK: Then did you write, "Dear Diary"? And we're also going to use "Well/ I've had my drink/(of tea)." Were those written near the same time?

ENSLIN: Yeah. Quite near.

NOWAK: Then, I know the next piece I've got . . . and you told me the story of this yesterday, but maybe we could just get it on tape . . . is, we're going to use the complete small piece, "In the Keepers House."

ENSLIN: Yeah. Okay, well we had a friend, who used to teach at Orono, and . . . but he was sort of in and out, and he seemed to have great luck in finding wealthy dowagers who would sort of lend him their houses. And it (laughs), he lived in some pretty surprising places. I used to call him the American Rilke, because Rilke was always, you know the *Duino Elegies.* Princess Maria Thurn und Taxishohenlohe owned Duino, which was a castle which was destroyed in the Second World War. But that's where Rilke was, when . . . well they'd just say "come on in (laughs), make yourself at home." And this guy was very much the adept at that kind of thing. He lived in this particular woman's house first, and then she was connected with a town organization which had bought the keeper's house connected with the Pemaquid light.

NOWAK: The what light?

ENSLIN: Pemaquid. P-e-m-a-q-u-i-d. It's down below Damariscotta, and he invited us down. The *pro-viso* was that he would live there. He would not have visitors. He would not use the phone . . . he would not do a lot of things, and he just sort of said "To hell with it!" and broke the lock off the phone. (laughs) And we stayed there, and this little collection of poems came very quickly. I never thought too much of it until a lot later. And I thought, "Well, not that bad," but it's about the house, about the fog bell outside. I think I have the dates of the founder, the foundry and the whole thing. That was that.

NOWAK: And that was one of the first ones that [Michael] Tarachow published, right?

ENSLIN: No, no.

NOWAK: Oh. That was a Salt-Works . . .

ENSLIN: That was Salt-Works. So what's his name, Tom Bridwell.

NOWAK: Okay. And that's when you first sort of early started that connection with him, and then he went on to publish a number . . .

ENSLIN: Yes. Oh, yes. Absolutely. He wrote to me. He was a friend of a former friend of mine on the Cape and he wrote to me and said, "Send me a little collection of poems and I can publish it in a week." (laughs) That isn't going to happen very many times, so I sent him that and he said, "Well, send me another one." And that was when I was as politically conscious as I ever was and I wrote something called *The Swamp Fox,* which was about General Francis Marion of the Revolution. And he did . . . I think those were the first two things he did, and then it got to other things. Some of them far more important including the first *important* one in my mind so far as the later musical experiments, which is *Carmina.* And thank god you pronounced it correctly. Everybody says "Carmeena," and it ain't! (laughs)

NOWAK: The next one that I took, and I think when I was going back, I think I told you I read through everything a couple of times, and I sort of made notes. And when I was first going through the first time, I read it and I think it was probably the first one that I put aside and said, "We gotta use this one total," was *Views,* which came out in '73.

ENSLIN: That's right.

NOWAK: And that was another one sort of like *The Poems* where it starts off "View from Olson's" and . . .

ENSLIN: Yes. Well I did a number of those. Many of which Jim Weil published in vastly overpriced editions. (laughs) And *Views* was the first one, and I got the idea of a sort of unity of my experiences. And so I would jot things down, "Okay, let's see what can I do from . . . I've been here," and that was all very conscious. The ordering of it was another thing because it wasn't consecutive. "Well I was here, and then I was here." And there is one thing interesting that was still, in the time when I was politically moved a little bit. I guess it was because of a number of things, the Vietnam thing. And I had just married a young wife who was certainly involved in all of this stuff. And there is one of them which is called "The View from Indian Island," and the view from Indian Island is the Penobscot Reservation of Old Town, Maine. And it was a very sad place, still is a sad place. And a "tribute" to the way in which treaties were kept, because by the original treaty, *all* of the river, *all* of the islands in the Penobscot River were given to the Penobscot Nation. And the only one they got was that one. That was published a number of times, and it was in newspapers. I made a sort of public statement. I guess I talked to Snyder, because he'd done some of those things. He said, "Well, just put it in public domain. Anybody can publish it anytime." And it was.

NOWAK: So it got reprinted a lot?

ENSLIN: Yes.

NOWAK: It seems one of the few pieces that really, to me when I read it . . . seemed consciously almost more like a visual artist. In terms of that they really were a series of perspective pieces of standing in this position, looking in this direction and then moving to this position, looking at that direction.

ENSLIN: Well, they were. I would say that I've done very few things like that, except for something that was never published. But Jim Weil was thinking of doing it: Areas, Districts, Environs. That's still in manuscript form if you want to dig it out from the chest. (laughs)

NOWAK: Oh, I don't know. Those are going right to Bertholf, those chests. Then I'll go to Buffalo, take one copy of everything out of there . . . we'll be set! Maybe I'll get my dad, he's retired now, to get one copy of each out of those chests. He's there at Buffalo. It'll be a little task for him for the winter.

ENSLIN: (laughs) The leg work!

NOWAK: That's right! The next one, and we took this one too complete, was *Fever Poems*. What's behind those?

ENSLIN: That was published by Gary Lawless, Blackberry [Press], and he wanted something, and those really were out of . . . I still don't know what was wrong with me. But I had, what in the old days used to be called an Intermittent Fever. In other words, every afternoon I would get a temperature that would shoot up, oh to about a hundred and three or something like that. And the next morning, I'd be . . . you'd feel the way you do feel after a fever, dry-mouth, but pretty much all right, and I'd think I was all right until it happened again. I never really had hallucinations, but I was somewhat out of it. Gary wanted them . . . wanted something to publish. And a number of afternoons while trying to control it but not quite able, and not really wanting to control everything because I was interested in what was sort of going on fuzzily, I lay out on the lawn at the house in Temple, and I wrote poems, and I never really much looked at 'em . . . And I called them *Fever Poems,* and I said "Do you want to publish these? Go ahead."

NOWAK: So they were all written in the state of fever?

ENSLIN: Yeah, they were.

NOWAK: Almost kind of like Dostoevsky you were working there. (laughs)

ENSLIN: Well, yeah, that title is exact.

NOWAK: Then we took . . . let's see, one, two, three, four pieces from *Ländler* which came out in '75.

ENSLIN: *Ländler,* okay. You know what a Ländler is? It is an Austrian dance. What it actually means is land dance. It's an Austrian peasant dance related quite closely to the waltz. It is in three-four time. It was used a great deal by symphonists of the nineteenth century. Bruckner wrote Ländler instead of scherzos. Mahler did some very famous ones. As a matter of fact, at the beginning of *Ländler,* there is . . . there are a couple of bars of music. Okay, that is the (sings) da da da dee da da dum bum ba dee da da da dee dum bum ba ba ba. That's the beginning.

NOWAK: Should we put that in the *Selected?*

ENSLIN: You could if you wanted to. Sure, go ahead. It's the beginning of the Ländler of the Second Symphony of Mahler. Something that I've loved ever since I was fifteen.

NOWAK: And then I'll just go through the poems, and if anything comes to your mind about them, just let me know. First one was "The First Horse Prayer" which I wrote to you [about], and we couldn't figure out where it was. I read it and you couldn't remember.

ENSLIN: "The First Horse Prayer." That has some funny things in it. That was when I was systematically reading sagas and the accounts of the horse sacrifice, and . . .

NOWAK: Icelandic sagas, or?

ENSLIN: Yes. Icelandic Sagas. They were sacrifices to Thor, which is actually illegal now. But there is a guy in Iceland that's trying to bring back the cult of Thor. (laughs) The supplicants go up to stone altars at night and they sacrifice horses. And they take blood and smear it on gold arm rings. (laughs)

NOWAK: I think [Robert] Kelly would probably be the only one who would know about that. (laughs)

ENSLIN: Exactly. *He told me!* And then I found it, and this guy really is out there. As a matter of fact, Howard [McCord], when he went to Iceland, found out some stuff about it. But anyway. I really hadn't thought of writing a poem until talking with Alison's mother, who is a horse person. And I (laughs) told her about the horse sacrifices, (laughs) and she was horrified. And then she said, "Well did you ever write a poem about horses?" And I said, "Not as such. I guess horses have appeared . . . okay. I'll write you a horse poem." (laughs) And I did. I gave it to her and I think she was a little puzzled. (laughs)

NOWAK: I bet she was puzzled. Not a living horse poem!

ENSLIN: (laughs) No!

NOWAK: Then I also took "I, Too, Chief Joseph."

ENSLIN: "I, Too, Chief Joseph." Of course Chief Joseph of the Nez Perce. My admiration is . . . for many that very touching last speech. The way in which he conducted himself during the whole thing. And later on . . . I read a number of those Native American orators. Luther Standingbear, I was very much impressed with him.

NOWAK: And there was, actually, that was a period when you were working with some Native American materials, right? There was a poem in *Views*. This piece . . . there was a little later I think, *The Fifth Direction* where you were you dealing with that . . .

ENSLIN: Yes. Exactly. That was all when I was going to the southwest very much, very often. And I was very much impressed with it. I was influenced, but at the same time, Keith Wilson, who is native, said, "Well, you're doing it right . . ."

NOWAK: Native to the southwest?

ENSLIN: Yes, he is native to the southwest. ". . . You're not trying to become what you are not." And I said, "No, this is not my heritage, but I feel a response to it."

NOWAK: So you're not becoming, like Gary Snyder . . .

ENSLIN: No, I am not!

NOWAK: Or Jerry [Rothenberg], where he shakes the rattles and sings!

ENSLIN: Exactly. I simply can't do that. But I can respond. And the culmination of that was in a section of something that is not in this at all. There is a section of *Ranger*, quite a late one, called "Peña Blanca," and that is as close to enlightenment as I ever came . . .

[TAPE BREAK]

NOWAK: What about . . . there were two poems from *Ländler*, "I said . . ." and "The American Dream." I especially remember "The American Dream."

ENSLIN: "The American Dream." That was a bitter one. (laughs)

NOWAK: Yep.

ENSLIN: "And I want no part of it." And I almost . . . you know, Jim Weil is a pretty uptight business man type. (laughs) And, I didn't know whether he'd go for that. I don't know whether he even read it, except to proof read it. (laughs)

NOWAK: Now, it sort of works out nicely how we're beginning a new tape here as well, because we're at *Carmina,* which is sort of a break and a changing point.

ENSLIN: Okay. That was the real beginning, I didn't quite understand what it was when I wrote it, but I liked it. The Latin simply means songs. And I read sections of it at a private reading in a house in South Harpswell, which is near Brunswick, where Gary Lawless and his girlfriend lived . . . Jim Koller was there. A couple of other people, and I . . . *Carmina* was, I'm not sure whether it had been published or whether it was just going to be. Anyway. It was the first time that I had read from it and I stopped at one point and said, "You know, there is a real sense of counterpoint in this," which I did not realize when I did it. That is, you could read, I think it's something like seventeen, nineteen, eighteen, twenty. About six of those. If you read, say seventeen and nineteen simultaneously, they really work. And so good accurate Koller who is always . . . he tries to be the . . . (laughs)

NOWAK: He's always at the ready.

ENSLIN: Yeah. He's always at the ready. He's a sort of a maverick Jimmy Stewart. Don't say much, but it's all . . . "Well, why don't we do it." So we did, and it did work. And yeah, well now I really am using some of these musical things that I had been thinking about. And there's an answer . . . The real reason that I went to see Conrad Aiken in the first place was because he had written a series of essays, early ones, in a book called *Skepticisms,* which by the way is a good collection. Some of his prose is a lot better than his poetry. But he was talking about counterpoint and poetry and blah blah blah blah blah, and I went and talked to the man and it was quite obviously . . . he wasn't thinking that way at all. But he was using that loose phraseology which many poets have when they talk about their ear and the . . . and using strict musical terms. The cadence again. That whole idea, I got pretty fed up with it. But I realized, well okay here's an answer to the old walrus. I really did do some counterpoint here.

NOWAK: So there was sort of a period up to . . . like you said before, up to *To Come To Have Become.* Then there was this period up to *Carmina,* and then *Carmina* kind of signaled the beginning of the newer kind of work. I know that I kept some notes. And I would take those big post-it notes and I'd just jot a phrase or something down each time I read a book, through these works, trying to make decisions. And for this one, that's what I put down, that you really get a sense, that this is, you know, the first step toward *Music for Several Occasions,* or something like that. It's just, there's a really strong sense of that.

ENSLIN: Exactly. It was a place where I first started thinking about things, and thinking that maybe I could take actual musical forms, being very careful. I guess this was still an Olsonian idea, the idea of organic form, which was nothing new to me. When Olson first started talking about it, I said to Cid, when the first draft of "Projective Verse" came out, "Well yeah, this is all very true, but you know, if Charles had ever analyzed a Haydn quartet, he wouldn't have had to have written it. Of course it's organic form!" All this bullshit the musicologists talk about as sonata form and so forth and so on, and they make this big spiel about ironclad forms, mold, cookie cutter. Those guys, Haydn and Mozart and the rest of them, wouldn't have known what was meant by sonata form. They thought that way, and thinking that way the form can be quite similar in some ways, and yet if you really analyze a particular piece, you find, no, it's the *material* that says, "Okay. You do it this way. This is what is here." And this was something that I wanted to explore. I felt that if I did that, I would have to use *specific* pieces, that is if I was going to do a Rondo, as I later did, I would take a particular Rondo. I would not simply say, "Well, a Rondo is an embellished melody, usually used in the last movement," blah blah, blah, blah, blah.

NOWAK: So you would go to a specific composition.

ENSLIN: So in that case I went to a specific composition, which I inflicted on you (laughs), and I did it in a number of other places. In *Casebook* there is a very good example in the "Sonata for a Sextet." And that is the Opus 18 of Brahms, and I swear I could . . . I don't know whether I could still do it, but when I got done with that thing, I think I could have written that score backwards. I really studied it. (laughs) I'm gonna get this now!

NOWAK: What about . . . then I think from *Carmina*, which came out in '76, we jumped to . . . I jumped up to 1980, with *The Flare of Beginning is in November*, which is a book of small pieces. But the reason I liked that is that it seemed to take the *Carmina* musical sense, but it seemed really, where that seemed a little more melodic, this one seemed more percussive. It was a really kind of crisp piece.

ENSLIN: Okay. There is a series of twelve of those month things. Some of them were published, some of them were not. And I had fun doing them. That one was . . . that was done by . . . who was it?

NOWAK: Jordan Davies?

ENSLIN: Jordan Davies. Right. It's very nicely printed, as a matter of fact. Yeh, I kind of liked that myself.

NOWAK: Did you write the month pieces in the months? Did you write this piece in November?

ENSLIN: I can't remember. Probably not.

NOWAK: What about *Two Geese,* which is just a beautiful little . . .

ENSLIN: *Two Geese.* Well that was . . . yes.

NOWAK: Do you remember writing that one?

ENSLIN: Yeah. I remember writing that one. Yes, actually, the two cognates and it was both sides of the house. I saw geese through those windows [points to the front kitchen window], and then I opened the back door and there I saw another one. (laughs) That's how it happened. (laughs)

NOWAK: So it was at this house?

ENSLIN: It was at this house. Those windows, that door.

NOWAK: What about *September's Bonfire,* which is a piece that you decided to read at Orono last year [National Poetry Foundation's "Poets of the 1950s" Conference, at which Enslin was a keynote reader].

ENSLIN: Yeah I did, didn't I? Well that was another one in the months. And I was playing there with the whole idea of Bone Fire. *Bon feu,* which is the French "good fire," and just having fun with it. Well, the four people became . . . were a little more conscious of what they were doing. (laughs) That was the season, when people start burning leaves, and clearing up the debris from the winter, and . . .

NOWAK: Was that, were any of the pieces there . . . Did you have any specific musical compositions in mind with the movement of language?

ENSLIN: Not . . . not specifically as such. But by that time I was so saturated with all of this that I undoubtedly felt something from specific sources. And I guess it was Metcalf that said, "Well you know you're talking about all this music. I just don't get it. I don't see that there's any of that. I like those little poems. They don't have anything to do with music." And I said, "If you really look carefully at the ones that happen before I became very much involved in this, and you looked at superficially similar ones that still occur, I think you'll find quite a difference."

NOWAK: And don't you think Metcalf says that but he thinks otherwise? Because he likes Ives.

ENSLIN: Well yes. He wants to bait you! He wants to get all he can out of it. (laughs) Of course he does, sure.

NOWAK: Because his pieces are as organized . . .

ENSLIN: Yes. I know.

NOWAK: . . . in that way as anybody else.

ENSLIN: Right.

NOWAK: What about the little book Karl Young put out . . . and this might have been the first Karl Young book of yours. Was it *Markings?*

ENSLIN: No, that wasn't the first one.

NOWAK: Well . . . what did that grow out of? Was that . . .

ENSLIN: I can't remember.

NOWAK: Was that . . . sort of archeological? Making marks and . . .

ENSLIN: Yes. As I told you, I can't remember every thing, and I don't remember too much about that one except that he did do it. And then, right after that he did my *tour de force*, which is *Opus O*.

NOWAK: What about with *Markings* . . . It seemed to me a little bit, almost like *Views,* in that it's sort of marking a spot and then looking from a particular position, it seemed a sort of perspective piece.

ENSLIN: Oh! I know! I know something about this. There is a poem, I think it's in *With Light Reflected,* called "X Marks the Spot," in which a rather factual account of a hangover, (laughs) "X Marks the Spot." And I'm thinking of the spot. The spot is marked, and from that, somehow it's a sort of expanding, and I got to this idea of markings, and that was it.

NOWAK: So it sort of grew out of *With Light Reflected* which is what, '70 something that's quite a while before that, wasn't it early '70s?

ENSLIN: Yeah, quite a year.

NOWAK: Then I put down *To Come Home (To),* which I remember when reading it, I think I marked down, where I kept my little notes, that it sort of grew out of the Bucolics.

ENSLIN: That is the book that we were talking about last night. It was. It was both that, and it was an answer, not wholly kind, to the place where Snyder attempted Haiku. The so called Hitch Haiku, and . . .

NOWAK: Hitch Haiku?

ENSLIN: In the first place I am not satisfied that you can write genuine Haiku in English at all. You can write pithy little poems and you can use seventeen syllables and you can do all kinds of things, but it doesn't seem to me that it is necessarily Japanese Haiku. Yes, that is the one that has the advice to the game warden.

NOWAK: Right. That's the one. Well . . . because you know I read that and I was reading it and I marked down the note to myself of how it sounded like some of the Greek Bucolics: Theocritus, Bion, etc. And there seemed to be a connection . . .

ENSLIN: It does. It does.

NOWAK: And then you mentioned in the note at the back of it that you had been doing some translating, I think, at that time. Is that about when that Salt-Works book of translations came out?

ENSLIN: Yes. The Pindarius Epigrammata, which was the fragments of Pindar, and the entire epigrams Callimachus, right.

NOWAK: And it seemed like . . . that there had been an influence in reading and attempting to translate that type of poetry at the time.

409

ENSLIN: There was, that's right, because neither Callimachus nor Pindar were Greek Bucolics, but it was from that. From the fact of doing those translations which was more or less actually a tribute to my father because . . .

NOWAK: Because you got all the Loebs from him.

ENSLIN: I inherited the Loebs from him. I had given him, actually, the copy of Pindar. And I thought, "Well, the old man might have liked this." I never have really done much translation. Let's see how good my Greek is. (laughs)

NOWAK: Well it was a unique book in that there isn't much else like that, that direct link. Then we've got complete *Music for Several Occasions*.

ENSLIN: Okay. There, of course, is the "Rondo." There is the first one, the . . .

NOWAK: The, "Chaconne," and there's a "Canzone" . . .

ENSLIN: No. What is the first one? Oh god . . .

NOWAK: I'll go look it up back there.

ENSLIN: I hate myself. (laughs) No, but I get that. I don't forget names, I don't forget things, but just something like that. It'll come to me in a minute. Anyway, that was the twelve houses on the road.

NOWAK: And where is that road? Let me go look it up.

ENSLIN: This road. Let's see what we've got here, "Chromatic Fantasy." And it was called a "Chromatic Fantasy" because of the Bach Chromatic fantasy, and also because if you are using a chromatic scale, you use all twelve tones. In other words, you would go from C to either C sharp, or D flat. Figuring in what your enharmonics are. Because ideally, C sharp and D flat are not the same tone. And you can make a difference with either a wind or a string instrument, you can't do it with a piano. (laughs) But that came from thinking of that and also thinking of the houses, the old houses on this road.

NOWAK: On the Kansas Road [where Enslin lives, in Milbridge, Maine]?

ENSLIN: On the Kansas Road, and there are twelve of them. This is one of them, they are all on . . .

NOWAK: Which one is this? Which number, coming up from this town?

ENSLIN: This would be three, so this would be D.

NOWAK: Living in D.

ENSLIN: Living in D. (laughs)

NOWAK: That could be a title of another book. (laughs)

ENSLIN: And then I became interested in the fact that the . . . our closest connections with people who lived in those houses were more or less like the closest connections between notes of a scale. In other words, if you go from C, the closest relation, if you're going to modulate, the easiest way to do it is by the so called "circle of fifths." Okay. So the Fifth, cutting out all the chromatics, the fifth is G. C to G. Okay. We are closest to the house which would correspond to G. Okay. The next one, the one by the way which would make the Plagal Cadence, is the . . . that's the dominant. Okay, tonic C, dominant G. Tonic C, subdominant is F. Same thing. That was the next closest, and it was pretty close, the connections, the whole way, and so I . . .

NOWAK: A lot of dissonance on the road? (laughs)

ENSLIN: A lot of dissonance, and I could set this up as a walk. I can have a hell of a lot of fun with it. As a matter of fact, I read that a couple of times, and the end it, because it does get into some . . . a little tongue twister device, and I think, "Well it was a long walk." (laughs)

NOWAK: Then what about . . . was it "Witch Hazel" that you said you had written in six minutes or something like that, and that's sort of the story behind the "Rondo" as well.

ENSLIN: The "Rondo" is seven minutes, and I know it because I thought it was going to be a very difficult thing to write, and I laid out—I was cleaned up a little bit (laughs) more up there, and the ships clock was running, so I know the time. I laid out sheets of paper all over that big desk and thinking, "Well I could put parts here." And I found that I did not need to do it. It just wrote itself. I didn't change a thing. It took exactly seven minutes. It takes almost as long to read it as it took to write . . . and part of the original manuscript, which I guess Berthof has, is even more illegible. I could hardly read it because it was written so fast. It just . . . "My god, there it is!" (laughs)

NOWAK: Do you usually write most of this stuff out by hand? And then type it?

ENSLIN: Everything.

NOWAK: What about some of these . . . There seems to be a break after the "Concerto for Solo Voices and Chorus." And then the pieces at the end seem to be a little bit different style.

ENSLIN: They're not.

NOWAK: "Baldwin Head" and the "Summer Song"?

ENSLIN: Those were the originals. Those were the ones where I really went into it. "Baldwin Head," you saw Baldwin Head.

NOWAK: We were there yesterday.

ENSLIN: And the popplestone and all of that. That was written . . . it's not exactly minimalism, but it was tending in that direction.

NOWAK: Not as much as minimalism as that beeper in my car. (laughs)

ENSLIN: (laughs) Anyway, that one, "Baldwin Head," yeah, I dated that. I wrote that in Tom Harner's house, which is why it says Lancaster,

Pennsylvania.

NOWAK: Even though Baldwin Head is just down the road!

ENSLIN: (laughs) Right! And "Summer Song," well . . . "Song in Being."

NOWAK: One of them is dedicated to Janet Rodney right?

ENSLIN: That's it. Right. That's the one. Anyways, those were all written in a period of about six days. Yes.

NOWAK: All of them were, in Lancaster.

ENSLIN: No. I was on the road. I wrote that one in Lancaster. I wrote "Summer Song" on a Greyhound bus, and (laughs) "Song in Being" I guess I wrote at Keith's. I don't know, it was somewhere. But I like those a lot because I'm sort of saying to myself, "Now I'm wholly aware of what I'm doing and what I want to do."

NOWAK: So it took about ten years? From *Carmina* to this book to really . . .

ENSLIN: Yeah, just about. Just about. And in this one, that music is my own. (laughs)

NOWAK: Is it? That was done at Bowling Green. Then the next is the John Taggart favorite, *The Weather Within.*

ENSLIN: Yep. The Weather Within.

NOWAK: For Oppen.

ENSLIN: For Oppen. Okay. I'm using musical things. I am consciously taking George . . .

NOWAK: The gap syntax?

ENSLIN: That was the first time that gap syntax . . . that I used gap syntax, and I did it primarily at least at the beginning of this because he used it, and I tried to use it in a similar way. I don't know whether he would've really thought that or not. Then when I took it over, maybe I understood it better because I had been using it so much in that book. I realized, "No I don't want to do exactly what George did. There are other things that I can do with it, and it's a very useful tool. Thank you George, I'll take it!" I took from many many poems of George, things . . . in a number of cases, I even quarreled with him. You say this, but on the other hand, you know you mean this, and it was very similar to many conversations that we had on many subjects. We would talk that way. Back and forth. It was a very serious talk, because we were very serious craftsmen, and I had wanted . . . I had started that. Actually the dates on that . . . I think the dates were included on that book . . . but no, actually, a few of them were quite a bit earlier. And I had hoped to do the whole thing, finish it and give it to him, and then he died . . . .

NOWAK: Homage piece.

ENSLIN: Homage piece, yep. And that was . . . that's the story there . . . And at the same time I am using the musical stuff. When Taggart wrote his critique in "The Open Letter," he sent it to me first. And for about three minutes when I started reading it, I was a little bit annoyed, and I would've been . . . (laughs) "Don't tell me how I wrote or what I did." (laughs) And then I thought, "But yes, he's absolutely right. This is what I did. And this is why I did it." There was only one thing that when I wrote back [phone rings/pause in tape] . . . the only thing that I told him that he should've included in that, he did later, the section in which the bell figures, because the bell really *is* ringing. That is ringing the changes, and it's from a line, I think it's in *Of Being Numerous.* I'm not sure, but . . . so I was very much pleased to find that he liked it, and just sorry that I couldn't give it to George.

NOWAK: What about . . . three to go. *Casebook,* which was the one that you assigned for our class at Bowling Green. We're gonna use "Part Songs," which we did in Bowling Green, and that's the most, or one of the most, performative/scored pieces.

ENSLIN: Well, that was the beginning of yes . . . no . . . I've done other things like that. Yes that was . . . and I kept the sense of this, I . . . that took me longer to write than a lot of . . . quite a period of time. I took the title again from a completely musical source, the series of "Part Songs" of Mendelssohn, and decided that I could make a sort of caesura in the middle of the line, and maybe if I was fortunate and kept the continuity enough through that, it could be performed in a great number of different ways. It could be read straight. It could be read, the first part of a line could be read straight down, and then when you got to the end, you could start back and you could keep this thing going endlessly. You could read, as in those sections of *Carmina,* there are some sections, particularly, where you can read parts together, parts of lines together, parts of . . . you can take sections, complete sections and two or three can be read at the same time.

NOWAK: Taggart's got a piece like that. Is it "Body and Soul" for two readers?

ENSLIN: "Body and Soul." Yeah. Right.

NOWAK: That he did with [Ted] Pearson I think the first time.

ENSLIN: Yep. Yep. I did not by the way know about that piece at the time that I wrote this. Now when did I write that? Uh . . . it must have been . . .

NOWAK: The book came out in '87.

ENSLIN: Okay, and I was sixty in '85. Okay, so I started that in late '84 and I know this because I had my ear pierced for my sixtieth birthday, and I had it done three months before. I had that surgical steel plug in there, but (laughs) it got infected, it was swelling, and I was trying to write one of the sections of this. And so that's how you can date that one!

413

NOWAK: And then the "Motet," was that also based on a particular motet?

ENSLIN: The "Motet" is based on the very famous "Jesu, meine Seele" of Bach. (singing) "Jesu, meine . . ."

[TAPE BREAK]

ENSLIN: Though I set it up more like a Bach Cantata, that is with a Recitative, Conductus, the Duets and the various things, it does follow pretty much as if you listen to "Jesu, meine" . . . You will find that it is quite close.

NOWAK: Then we are using both halves of *Love and Science,* which are . . .

ENSLIN: Oh yes! (laughs) That *Love and Science* thing came out of an interest which was sparked first by Ivan Tolstoy, who came here and was talking about chaos, chaos as a theory. And the way in which he talked about it fascinated me because these apparently arbitrary happenings which you cannot predict in any way were happening in the work that I was doing. I mean I would find these variables . . . because some of the stuff really had been worked out mathematically. I wished many times while I was doing some of the stuff that I'd paid more attention to pure mathematics when I was a kid. And the only reason I didn't, I guess, was because I was in rebellion against my father who was trying to ram it down my throat! (laughs) But it would've been a lot easier. But I did find that in many cases where I thought, "Well yes, sure. You do this, you do this, you do this and this is what you're going to get," it didn't happen. And I'd go back and say, "It's gotta happen that way." And it didn't happen. There is the variable which is present, and so I talked to Ivan and I said, "I'm not going to understand all of this, but please, in as simple scientific terms as you can, try to explain some of this to me and I'll tell you why when you get done." And I took in as much as I could follow. "That is precisely the experience that I'm having." And so I sort of hit on it. Okay. It's a sort of sequence. A lot of people have not liked it, thought it was too austere, and it is austere in a way. Some people have. Anyway, it wasn't quite long enough for a book and I was playing around with a series of sort of Neo-Classic poems. Sort of reminiscent in some ways of the Cavalier poets and guys like that. As a tribute to Alison I was thinking of music again in that I was thinking of Stravinsky's experiments with it. That is the ballet *Pulcinella*, which is probably the first full fledged Neo-Classic thing which comes to mind in music, as Bach with wrong notes. (laughs) And this modelled on, you know, the Cavalier period, but it's not. There are some things here that are pretty contemporary, and instead of going through stages . . . The thing that is so evident in Neo-Classicism, in Picasso at the same period, those faces in which you've got all three dimensions flattened out into one, but that's exactly what. Okay. In *Pulcinella*, Stravinsky takes those Pergolesi melodies, but where the conventions of the early eighteenth century would've been to have done a tonic dominant sub-dominant, the very logical thing, no, he doesn't do that at all. He just lays the whole thing out flat. The melody is there, and underneath this the modulations are all laid out in a line. They're all one, so that there are all these crazy dissonances that you get. A lovely melody, (sings) da dee da da da da dee da, da dee da da da da da da. And instead of having merely the conventional melody, you get these quite strange sounds against them. Of course I've stolen things like that. "The Unanswered Question" is a perfect example of that. That was Neo-Classicism before there was Neo-Classicism. He didn't know what the hell it was. But it sounded good, and he did it well! (laughs)

NOWAK: Is Ivan . . . is Leo's grandson, or great grandson?

ENSLIN: Grandson. Youngest grandson.

NOWAK: Then we've got, to end the *Selected* off, the two triptychs, "Triptych 1990" and "Triptych 1991." What's the idea behind those pieces?

ENSLIN: They were actually my first real experiments . . . they weren't experiments exactly, but the first use of the elements that I can use from minimalism in which there is this apparent repetition which is not repetition in the least. And it goes back to something that impressed me very much when I first read it in René Char, in a book called *Hypnos Waking*, which is about 1960 I guess. And what he says is the act, even if it is repeated, is always virgin, and . . .

NOWAK: Which is Schoenberg's theory of variation.

ENSLIN: That's exactly right.

NOWAK: Repetition and variation.

ENSLIN: Absolutely. And so called minimalism is simply an extension of the same thing. Anyway, the first one, [from] "Triptych 1990," is "Aberrant Rock" which you published in *furnitures*. That's developed in one way and I had great fun in doing it, and as I told Carolyn [Erler], "If you want to climb Burke Hill there, it's a little obscure to get in, but it's a nice walk when you get up there." And I said, "But of course I could tell you, as I told everyone else, you don't need to go up there. All you gotta do is read my poem. It's all there." (laughs)

NOWAK: And then what about the other pieces in there? "La Folia" you talked about.

ENSLIN: "La Folia," my life-long interest in La Folia, and more or less a tribute to the great number of composers over the years, right down to the twentieth century. Rachmaninoff, for instance, he used it, you know, in something that is called "Variations on a Theme of Corelli." Well it's not a theme of Corelli's. Corelli stole it the same as everybody else did. That's it. Then Carl Nielsen and Martinu. Martinu used it twice, Fifth and Sixth Symphony, and somebody very recently has used it. Somebody we both know . . . Penderecki.

NOWAK: Okay, and . . . how about "It Takes Me Some Time."

ENSLIN: "It Takes Me Some Time." Okay. "It Takes Me Some Time" is the third of the 1991. That came from an actual occurrence. Allen Ginsberg was at the National Poetry Conference, or what ever the hell that thing was called, in 1973. It was set up at a college that no longer exists, Grand Valley State in Michigan, very close to Grand Rapids. I think the college itself no longer even exists. But anyway, a gentleman by the name of Robert Vas Dias was there and he got this idea of getting together all the old objectivists who were still around for the last time, and people who in one way or another, in various generations, had been influenced by them.

NOWAK: So who did that include then? Oppen?

ENSLIN: It included Oppen, Reznikoff, Rakosi. Yeah, they were the beginning. And Duncan. Ed Dorn I never understood because I don't think you can put him with them. But anyway, he was there. Allen, and that does make some sense because Zukofsky was invited, but he wouldn't come because he was mad at Oppen. (laughs)

NOWAK: Some things never change.

ENSLIN: Some things never change. Duncan, Dorn . . .

NOWAK: Creeley?

ENSLIN: No. He'd had another festival a couple years before. Kelly and Diane Wakoski and that whole group was there. I was there, Diane Di Prima, George Economou, Rochelle Owens. (laughs) She gave a reading, and Reznikoff came up to me . . . "That was vicious!" (laughs)

NOWAK: So then there was this interchange, right? Between . . .

ENSLIN: Okay. Allen decided to do a sort of a blues improvisation. That's what he called it.

NOWAK: With harmonium?

ENSLIN: He sat there with a harmonium, and what he did was to throw out a line to all of us in a series, and we were supposed to answer him in rhyme. Well he'd done a couple and he got to Reznikoff, and Reznikoff (laughs) he looked like a little turtle. Very old, quite fat, bald head down like this. (laughs) He looked at him. He was half asleep. He was eighty - two, three at the time. And Allen said, "Mmmmm, old sage Reznikoff, how are you at rhyme?" "Very very good, but it takes me some time."

(laughs) It just cracked the place up (laughs) because it was not . . . there was no hesitation. (laughs) It was great!

NOWAK: So that stuck in your head for like fifteen, twenty years?

ENSLIN: Oh yeah! Yeah, right. And so when I was doing that, boy that would make . . . of course that one has very varied things in it. The second one is the "Rhyme of the Ancient Mariner." And anyway, that was how that happened. (laughs) And it really, [clock chimed twice in the background] it almost shut Allen up. And it was so good! I mean he did go on anyway, but boy . . .

NOWAK: There was a pause. (laughs)

ENSLIN: There was a pause. Good for you! (laughs)

NOWAK: What about, in terms of, like a larger picture, because we've gone through all the poetry that's going to be in here. If someone asked you, someone else was interviewing you and I know it's been framed in a lot of different ways, but kind of your . . . what you've given to contemporary poetry, or how you should be looked upon. I know, like Ed Foster's always saying that you're the modern Thoreau or something like that . . .

ENSLIN: Well, I really disclaim that because certainly Thoreau has been very important to me. I admire him greatly. I also admire greatly, and I tried to tell Ed that, at the end of *Walden* he says, "What I require of any man is that he give me a true and honest account of his life, and if there is that, it must have been in a very different country than the one that I occupied." And that makes pretty good sense. I mean yeah, I think he knew how to live and he did it and that's it. My hat's off to you. Some of the things I agree with heartily. On the other hand, there are places where I wouldn't want to go that way at all. So I, in a way, simply because I live in the sticks, am not particularly a Thoreau. Yes, I like doing it. I have done it most of my life and I hit on a way of survival early. Certainly if I were to try to live in a city now, I don't think I'd get along very well and I know I wouldn't be very happy. That's all, and hell, no big deal.

NOWAK: So how should your work be characterized though? I mean, if someone's got to say . . . you know, do one of those literary biographies . . .

ENSLIN: I don't know. Perhaps the emphasis on a unity of . . . a unity in craft with music, because I suppose in a sense that people say that I'm a . . . try to say to me sometimes, "Oh what a bully Nadia Boulanger was to tell you not to compose." And that's bullshit because I had come to the same conclusion. It was simply that she affirmed something that I already knew, and I was prepared to do it. Yes, it was shattering. Yes, I did not want to do it, but I realized that I should do it. And the way she put it when she said, "You are literate. You should write." And I think, though we had almost

417

no contact after that, I saw her once before she went back to France, an
. . . oh yes, I saw her once at the Longy School and we had a long talk afte
that but . . . and I dedicated the last, the coda of *Forms* is dedicated to he
I sent it to her and she sent me a very nice letter. But I've often said that
like to be considered as a composer who happens to use words instead c
notes. That's all. That is, if you want to flatter me, say that. Don't call m
a poet. Don't call me a writer. Don't call me . . . anything. Composer. I lik
the sense, because a composer we have associated completely with music
but there's no reason that we should. To compose is to put things togeth
er, and okay, well, writers do that just as well as composers. So I don
know, I don't mind Ed Foster. Again his insistence that I exemplif
Melopoeia in Pound's . . . I would hope that maybe Pound would thin
that. That Pound certainly had the ear for it, though he didn't have th
training. (laughs) Or like Achilles Fang always says, "Oh yeah, I taugh
Ezra all the Chinese he never knew."

NOWAK: Then what about the relationship to Maine landscape, Maine geog
raphy?

ENSLIN: Maine Landscape. Maine Geography. Okay. That of course is evi
dent, but it is quite incidental and I object to the usual sort of regional
ism. Okay, yeah I dig the place. I live here, and there are a lot of trees an
rocks and the sea and all of that, but if I . . . I've said many times if I ha
lived in a completely different place, completely different milieu, I'm con
vinced that I would have tried to have used everything that was there i
exactly the same way. And sometimes that upsets people.

NOWAK: So these things become elements in a composition.

ENSLIN: Exactly.

NOWAK: And that driving force is the composition, and that's sort of like
vacuum and it pulls . . .

ENSLIN: That is it. Yet on the other hand, never a complete reliance on tech
nique or craft. Yes, it's very important and it is the unifying force, but I an
not regional, certainly, in the usual sense . . . but I am very local. Most o
what I use is directly around me.

NOWAK: You could probably hike to most of it.

ENSLIN: Yeah. I can! (laughs) It's like having four addresses, all of them in th
same town. This one, Bloomside, the cove and the island. (laughs) It's a
in Milbridge.

NOWAK: It's all there. Anything else to add? Anything else you can think of

ENSLIN: No. I think we've covered it pretty well.

NOWAK: Okay, why don't I pop this off and . . .

ENSLIN: Is that okay with you . . .

LISTING OF ORIGINAL PUBLICATIONS

The Work Proposed. Ashland, MA: Origin Press, 1958.

New Sharon's Prospect. Ashland, MA: *Origin*, Second Series #7, 1962.

The Place Where I Am Standing. New Rochelle, NY: The Elizabeth Press, 1964.

This Do & The Talents. Mexico: Ediciones el Corno Emplumado, 1966.

To Come   To Have Become. New Rochelle, NY: The Elizabeth Press, 1966.

The Diabelli Variations & Other Poems. Annandale-on-Hudson, NY: Matter Books, 1967.

Agreement, and Back. New Rochelle, NY: The Elizabeth Press, 1969.

The Poems. New Rochelle, NY: The Elizabeth Press, 1970.

The Country of Our Consciousness. Berkeley, CA: Sand Dollar, 1971.

In the Keeper's House. Dennis, MA: Salt-Works Press, 1973.

Views. New Rochelle, NY: The Elizabeth Press, 1973.

Fever Poems. Brunswick, ME: Blackberry, 1974.

Ländler. New Rochelle, NY: The Elizabeth Press, 1975.

Carmina. Dennis, MA: Salt-Works Press, 1976.

The Flare of Beginning is in November. Brooklyn, NY: Jordan Davies, 1980.

Two Geese. Markesan, WI: Pentagram Press, 1980.

September's Bonfire. Needham, MA: Potes & Poets Press, 1981.

Markings. Milwaukee, WI: Membrane Press, 1981.

To Come Home (To). Fort Kent, ME: Great Raven Press, 1982.

Music for Several Occasions. Milwaukee, WI: Membrane Press, 1985.

The Weather Within. Milwaukee, WI: Membrane Press, 1985.

Case Book. Elmwood, CT: Potes & Poets Press, 1987.

Love and Science. Kenosha, WI: Light and Dust Books, 1990.

"Aberrant Rock" first appeared in *furnitures*.

"Word/Logos" first appeared in *:that:*.

"La Folia" first appeared in *lift*.

"Abendmusik," "More than Smoke this Water" and "Small Pastoral Displaced" first appeared in the *Light and Dust @ Grist Mobile Anthology of Poetry*.

INDEX OF BOOKS, TITLES, AND FIRST LINES

Books are indicated by bold typeface. Titles of individual poems are shown in all capital letters, and first lines in upper/lower case.

unto a song   that song's silence, 255

Warmth to come home, 36
Water, 96
Well, / I've had my drink / (of tea), 89
Went there swimming, 109
What can I taste?, 126
What do I hear?, 125
What falls/, 55
Whatever I hear from the high-flying / geese, 169
Whatever it was I heard in my head, 94
Whatever the pull, 103
Whatever winter flow, 197
What has moved us, moves most, 241
What I see first is, 112
What use in August?, 209
Wheat, and a river is it?, 17
Whenever I / consider, 212
When gulls / and ducks, 93
When I look up / I see, 126
Wherever there are lilacs, 202
Will the dreams make whole, 127
Will we be here, 235
WITCH HAZEL, 18
WORD/LOGOS, 362